D1335325

# Guarding
# Children's
# Interests

rdians

edings

LIBREX

# Guarding Children's Interests

## The Contribution of Guardians *ad Litem* in Court Proceedings

Jean McCausland

Edited by Annie Bourton

With editorial assistance from Kate Wilson

The
Children's
Society

A Voluntary Society of The Church of England and The Church in Wales

© The Children's Society 2000

First published in 2000

The Children's Society
Edward Rudolf House
Margery Street
London WC1X 0JL

A catalogue record of this book is available from
the British Library.

ISBN 1 899783 35 0

Cover photograph modelled for The Children's Society.

# *Contents*

# Foreword

We live in times of change. We have moved not only into a new century but also a new millennium. It is an important moment to take stock of the future. Our immediate future is bound up in the current generation of children. Some of those children have parents who are unable to or, for many different reasons, are unfitted to care for them. Their welfare should be the concern of not only the agencies primarily required to look after them, but also of society in general. Those children also will grow to form part of our future.

The guardian *ad litem* service is of comparatively recent origin but it has made itself indispensable in the work it does on behalf of children who have the greatest need of help and who come before the family courts. From my experience over the whole life of the service, it has provided experienced and dedicated people who know how to speak to and listen to children, assess the situation usually in the midst of a plethora of conflicting information, and provide to the court at every level an impartial, detached though understanding and sympathetic evaluation of the child's needs and recommendations for the future. Quite simply, judges and magistrates would be in grave difficulties in making decisions about children in the absence of the guardian *ad litem* reports.

The Children's Society has played an extremely important part in the creation and continuing of the guardian *ad litem* service. It has managed one of the busiest panels in the country. It now has great experience of the working of the system. The research which it has commissioned provides for those dealing with children a most valuable insight into the working of guardians *ad litem*. It also provides a rare opportunity to find out the views of the children about the guardians, their own lawyers where they are old enough to instruct them, and the court process itself. It is particularly interesting that this research should have been concluded and this book published now, since the entire guardian service is about to undergo the enormous upheaval of integration into the Children and Family Court Advisory Service, coming into being in

April 2001. The implications of this research will have to be carefully considered as we all seek to provide a better service in and out of the courts for the children who are the subject of these proceedings.

In my view this is a book which ought to be on the bookshelves of all those engaged in child care matters which will or may go to court proceedings, in particular judges, barristers and solicitors as well as social work and health care professionals.

THE RT. HON. DAME ELIZABETH BUTLER-SLOSS, D.B.E.
President of the Family Division,
Royal Courts of Justice

# Preface

The guardian *ad litem* service was established in 1984, and consolidated and extended by the Children Act 1989. The service provided for the representation of children in public law proceedings by an independent person who had knowledge and experience of children, families and child protection services. Section 41 of the Children Act 1989 laid a general duty upon guardians *ad litem* to safeguard the interests of the child and a requirement to report to the court on whether the recommended order was likely to secure the welfare of the child in the light of all the available evidence and other possible orders.

Following a direct approach by the local social services department, The Children's Society's Guardian *ad litem* Project in Humberside was established in 1985 and became operational in 1986. This was the voluntary sector's first specialist guardian *ad litem* team and its findings were published in 1990 in a research report, *Speaking Out for Children*, by Joan Hunt and Mervyn Murch.

The Children's Society project continued to evolve, taking over management of the panel in 1992, now being one of five guardian *ad litem* and reporting officer panels in England and Wales managed by a voluntary agency. On 1 April 1996, with the abolition of Humberside as a local authority, the project negotiated four service level agreements whereby each of the four successor authorities – the City of Kingston upon Hull, East Riding of Yorkshire, North East Lincolnshire and North Lincolnshire – contracted the management of the service out to The Children's Society. The panel retains the original name.

The panel has been one of the busiest in England: in its peak year, 1994/95, guardians were appointed in 455 sets of proceedings involving 727 children. In 1998/99 there were new appointments in 318 sets of proceedings involving 502 children and 519 active cases involving 878 children.

The project sought further funding from The Children's Society to undertake some more research after the Children Act 1989. The original proposal for a Children's Society funded research post was specifically to undertake an evaluation of children and young people's perceptions of the guardian *ad litem* role using a non-abusive research framework. One of the purposes was to enable children and young people to influence decisions, systems and practices which affect their lives, consistent with The Children's Society's aims.

A decision was made during 1996 that the researcher would not be a guardian *ad litem*, to provide more objectivity, but that the person appointed would have experience of working with children and young people, and understand the ethical dilemmas of children and young people's involvement in research. The consent of the President of the Family Division was sought for the first research proposal on children's views and meanwhile a further piece of research was undertaken on professionals' view of the guardian *ad litem*'s contribution to care proceedings.

The researcher was an integral part of the panel management and administration and assisted with the collation of other data from the end of case forms completed by all guardians, for example substance abuse and domestic violence. It is a model that the project hopes can be retained in the future and perhaps developed in any new service.

As this research goes to press there is considerable discussion about the proposed new Children and Family Court Advisory Service (CAFCAS), planned for inauguration in 2001. We hope that findings in this research will assist with this development and enable children subject to proceedings to remain in focus.

JEAN MCCAUSLAND
ANNIE BOURTON

# *Acknowledgements*

The author would like to thank the many people who have made these two pieces of research possible.

Above all I owe thanks to the children and young people, social workers, local authority solicitors, children's solicitors, parents' solicitors and guardians who gave their valuable time to participate in my research studies. The interview and questionnaire responses were thoughtful and revealing. They shed light on the nature of the guardian *ad litem* role and its contribution to children caught up in public law proceedings and to child care practice in general.

My particular thanks to the Humberside GALRO Panel manager, Helen Van Greuning, who was responsible for developing the research itself. Her support, direction and encouragement were much valued during the initiation and conduct of these two pieces of research, as was the advice she gave based on her experience of the guardian *ad litem* service and child care practice.

Deliberations on the final questionnaire, interview schedule and research methodologies were stimulated by the advisory groups who provided advice based on their extensive experience of public family law proceedings and/or research. The members of the professionals' research advisory group were Jane Birkinshaw, Paul Dyson, John Hogg, Paul Newman, Ruth Turner and Sandra Twigger. The children's research advisory group consisted of Phil Burns, His Honour Judge Cracknell, Jenny Dagg, Dawn Hutchinson, Judith Knight, Ulric Murray, Jane Spiers, Sandra Twigger, Kate Wilson and Ken Wood.

From The Children's Society I would like to thank Gwyther Rees and Lorraine Wallis for their advice on qualitative analysis, and Lucy Kirkbride for suggesting that I use a board game in my interviews with children. Also, Nigel Hinks for his support whilst negotiating for permissions from the Lord Chancellor's Department.

Thanks to the guardians and administrators at the Humberside GALRO Panel office who have helped with proof reading and have given their advice, support and encouragement whilst undertaking the research studies.

My particular thanks to the guardian Annie Bourton for her editorial assistance in the final stages of writing up the report. Her extensive knowledge of the GALRO service, its history and proposed changes to the service was invaluable in identifying the implications of research findings and relating this to policy and GALRO practice. In addition, Annie assisted me to write some sections of the report and was responsible for writing the final chapter.

The Children's Society would like to thank the members of the Publications Advisory Group for their valued advice: Kathy Aubeelack; Nicola Baboneau; Ron Chopping (Chair); Annabelle Dixon; Sara Fielden; Judy Foster; Christopher Walsh.

JEAN McCAUSLAND

*1*

# Introduction and overview

## THE GUARDIAN *AD LITEM* SERVICE

The guardian *ad litem* service as it currently operates has its origins in the inquiry report written following the death of Maria Colwell in 1973. Maria had been returned to the care of her mother and stepfather under the auspices of a care order. When her mother applied for the revocation of this order, this was not opposed by the local authority who viewed the outcome as inevitable. Although made the subject of a supervision order, Maria was subsequently killed by her stepfather, having suffered severe neglect and emotional and physical harm prior to her death. The subsequent inquiry report stated: 'It would have been of assistance to the Court to have had the views of an independent social worker' (Department of Health and Social Security, 1974). The 'independence' was from the parents and the local authority, and introduced the concept of separate representation for the child in care proceedings. The legislation enabling this to happen, while contained in the Children Act 1975, was not fully implemented until 27 May 1984, when panels of guardians *ad litem* and reporting officers (GALROs) were established.

At that time guardians *ad litem* could be appointed in adoption, freeing for adoption, care and related proceedings including termination of access. The role of the reporting officer was introduced specifically to interview parents concerning their agreement to an adoption order and to see that consent was freely given, informed and unconditional. Local authorities had a duty to provide panels of guardians *ad litem* and reporting officers who would be independent of them, and from which the courts could make appointments. The informal, reciprocal arrangements between local authorities mostly developed into panels of self-employed fee-attracting guardians, or formal consortia arrangements between local authorities.

The structure enabled children to be independently represented, but while it was a significant step forward for children it had its limitations. The child's party status was discretionary and relied on the court ordering that the child be made a party to the proceedings. There remained other routes into the care system via matrimonial or wardship proceedings where the child had no possibility of party status.

The Children Act 1989, which was implemented in October 1991, extended the role of the guardian *ad litem* and also directed courts to appoint a guardian unless they were satisfied that it was not in the child's interest to do so. The primary duties of a guardian, which are set out in guidance for guardians and reporting officers (Department of Health, 1992), are:

- to safeguard the interest of the child (Children Act 1989, S41(2));
- to ensure the child has an effective voice in court by representing his or her 'ascertainable wishes and feelings' (Children Act 1989, S1(3)(a) as applied to the guardian by Family Proceedings Rules);
- to seek to avoid delays in a case being heard and determined (Children Act 1989, S1(2) and the Family Proceedings Rules as above);
- to have regard to the Welfare Checklist (Children Act 1989, S1(3)).

In addition, guardians attend all hearings and directions appointments (unless excused) and advise the court orally or in writing on:

- the child's level of understanding, e.g. consent or refusal to medical/psychiatric examination;
- the child's wishes on any issue, e.g. attendance at court;
- which tier of the court the case should be heard in and timetabling;
- options available to the court, their suitability, and what order if any should be made;
- any other matter on which the guardian's advice is sought.

In addition there is now an expectation that the guardian will chair meetings of expert witnesses with a view to a summary of agreed evidence being produced (Children Act Advisory Committee, 1997).

The child's party status is no longer discretionary: unless the court is satisfied that it is not necessary to do so to safeguard the child's interests, guardians will be appointed in the following proceedings (Children Act 1989, S41(6) and Rule 2 of the Family Proceedings Rules):

- any application for a care order or supervision order;
- any proceedings in which a court has made a direction under S37(1) and has made or is considering whether to make an interim care order;
- any application to discharge a care order or vary or discharge a supervision order;

- any application for a supervision order to be substituted for a care order;
- any case in which the court is considering whether to make a residence order for a child already subject to a care order;
- any case in which contact for a child on a care order is being considered;
- any application of a child assessment order;
- any application for emergency protection order;
- any appeal arising from any of these proceedings;
- any (civil) application for secure accommodation order;
- any application to change a child's surname or remove him or her from the jurisdiction while subject to a care order;
- any application to extend a supervision order; and
- applications for parental orders (S30, Human Fertilisation and Embryology Act 1991).

Response from the courts to the work of guardians has in general been positive (Social Services Inspectorate, 1990), but pressure on legal aid funds, escalating expenditure in public law proceedings, pressure to extend representation into private family law proceedings, and concerns about delays in making decisions about children in care proceedings have struck a cautionary note.

In the House of Lords in December 1996 Lord Irvine of Lairg, as shadow chancellor, raised the issue of whether dual representation of children by both a guardian and a solicitor was necessary, especially since the guardian and local authority were so often in agreement, stating: 'is it really necessary for the guardian to instruct ... another team of lawyers to put forward views which in most cases simply replicate the views of the local authority?' (Hansard, 1996) In the same period there were increasing debates about the spiralling legal aid bill in public law proceedings. One recurring issue was the high percentage of cases where the final recommendation by the guardian *ad litem* and the local authority were the same. Anecdotally both guardians themselves and their managers knew that to focus solely on the outcome was not telling the whole story of guardian involvement. At meetings with the Department of Health panel managers were advised to produce research that looked at the process and to move from anecdotes to evidence. At the time no major pieces of research on the issue of representation had been published, but in 1999 a cluster of research in response to these developments was published. This research contains a chapter on the legal representation of children in response to issues that arose during its course.

In a letter to all designated care judges in January 1998 Mr Justice Wall, a member of the Lord Chancellor's Family Law Advisory Board, asked for comments on the subject of representation in public law generally and about the relationship between the welfare role of the guardian and the legal function of the solicitor. He also asked whether there could be flexibility about the appointment of solicitors in all cases and whether the role of the guardian should be extended into private law, and how this could be achieved without detriment to the public law functions. This letter mirrored comments previously made by Geoffrey Hoon, the Lord Chancellor's parliamentary secretary, to a meeting on 3 November 1997, where he also indicated a full review of children's representation in family law proceedings. The review was announced by the Home Secretary on 16 February 1998 and a consultation into support services in family proceedings and the future organisation of court welfare services began. A consultation paper was published in July 1998 with responses to be returned by November 1998.

These developments highlighted the need for the guardian *ad litem* service to demonstrate the value-added contribution of guardians to the court process rather than a focus on outcomes alone. The research on professionals' views was commissioned in response to this need. As part of a children's organisation what we also wanted to do was to explore children's views of the service they were receiving, which was consistent with The Children's Society's aim of consulting with children on issues that affect their lives.

## REVIEW OF THE LITERATURE

The role of the guardian service in family proceedings is a relatively new one, and there have to date been few studies evaluating how it is operating or how the involvement of a guardian can change a case. A number of descriptive and guidance books for guardians *ad litem* have been written, including, for example, the *Manual of Practice Guidance for Guardians* ad Litem *and Reporting Officers* (Department of Health, 1992) and *The Work of the Guardian* ad Litem: *Practitioner's Guide* (Kerr and Gregory, 1998). The Department of Health has initiated a rolling programme of research to monitor the effectiveness of the Children Act 1989, including the work of guardians. In one such piece of commissioned research, Murch, Hunt and MacLeod (1990) recognise the difficulty on the part of the administering authorities in appraising the work of guardians. They acknowledge that although the guardian's work is under constant exami-

nation from solicitors, social workers and the court, neither court personnel nor solicitors (parents' and children's) are in a position to comment on
the whole of the guardian's practice. Social workers may feel that their
role constrains them from evaluating a guardian's performance. Children
and parents are the 'consumers' of the service yet they are largely
unheard. It then appears that one way of appraising the effectiveness of a
guardian's performance and the guardian service as a whole would be to
elicit the views of professionals and 'consumers'.

One of the first pieces of research to look at the operation of the
guardian service was commissioned by The Children's Society four years
after the guardian service was established and was based at the Humberside GALRO Panel (Hunt and Murch, 1990); the current piece of
research is an extension of this. In the first research, interviews were
undertaken with 11 guardians, 15 solicitors and key personnel in the
courts and Social Services as well as seven parents and seven children.
Hunt and Murch (1990) found that court personnel especially valued
guardians for their ability to be objective and child-focused in adversarial
proceedings. Solicitors valued guardians for the following reasons: their
ability to communicate with children; their knowledge of children's needs
and family history; and their access to information. Solicitors and
guardians valued each other's contribution in working together to represent the child. Social services staff welcomed the involvement of
guardians in care cases as they provided a second opinion, checked, challenged, or confirmed the actions of social workers. The parents interviewed were unclear as to the role of the guardian. Most thought the
guardian was a part of social services. The children were similarly confused about why the guardian was there and for whom he or she worked.
Every child stated that their guardian had been interested in what they
had to say. Less than half of the children thought that their guardian knew
them well enough to do a report on them. Since then, the Children Act
has been introduced (1991) and the role of guardians widened consider-
ably. This study provides useful information on the work of guardians as
perceived by professionals involved directly in care proceedings and the
'consumers' of these proceedings.

Among the recommendations to the Department of Health, Murch *et
al.* (1990) suggested the implementation of periodic appraisals and
reviews of guardians. There is now a statutory requirement (Regulation
10(1)) that each guardian's work is reviewed within their first year of an
appointment and s/he must be re-appointed at the end of each 3-year
period. The existing system of appraisal concentrates around the

guardian's final report and largely ignores the 'ongoing and intensive nature of involvement throughout the period of the court process', which is 'most important' (Timmis, 1996, p. 226). To correct this imbalance, Timmis conducted a small-scale study to give professionals an opportunity to comment on the process of guardian work. This study involved 82 cases and a range of professionals but no children.

Timmis found that guardians added value to proceedings by focusing on the child, providing a fresh view of a case and also expertise regarding issues in a case. The most commonly held 'useful' aspects of the guardians' involvement was their independent investigation and their support of social workers. Guardians were helpful in cases owing to their knowledge of the law, assisting parents to understand and accept the situation, and giving children a voice. Some guardians were seen as not useful because of their lack of involvement in cases, not being assertive or communicating clearly with other professionals. The majority of professionals viewed the relationship between the local authority and the guardian as professional and constructive or reasonably so. Most guardians were considered to be effective in their pursuit of the welfare of the child. There were six out of 82 cases where the individual guardian's performance was seen to be unhelpful or inadequate.

The validity of comments reported in Timmis' research is limited by a flawed sample selection procedure, since social workers, lawyers, guardians and magistrates were not randomly selected for inclusion in the study, but chosen on the basis of their acquaintance with the researcher. In addition, the professionals chose the cases on which they wished to complete questionnaires and it seems likely that they selected cases that were memorable because they were unusual rather than ones that were representative. Thus many seem to have chosen long, complex and adversarial cases, and cases where there had been disagreements between professionals. Despite these methodological problems, Timmis's research provides an indication of areas where guardians were seen to be effective and of added value to proceedings. It also adds to our limited knowledge of what guardians actually do throughout the court process as opposed to what should be done as set out in the Court Rules. Most importantly, the study highlights the need for methodologically sound research on professionals' views of the service in order to gain a clearer picture of the impact of a guardian's involvement throughout proceedings and identify aspects of a guardian's work that are seen to be effective.

Until recently research into the GALRO service has largely failed to take account of the views of children and young people represented by guardians. However, in the mid-1990s five studies (including this one) were initiated that looked specifically at the experiences and views of children: of these three have been published to date, the first by a guardian *ad litem*, Clark, in 1995, and more recently those by Masson and Winn Oakley (1999) and Clark and Sinclair (1999).

In Clark's study nine children aged between 8 and 18 years, 16 solicitors and 18 guardians were interviewed in order to examine the 'representational triangle' formed in public law proceedings by the older child, the guardian and solicitor. The professionals and children had been involved together in 29 proceedings. Clark found that many of the children had played no real part in their cases, did not attend court and were not clear about what had happened in the proceedings. The solicitors interviewed met only 35% of their child clients. The guardian told some solicitors that the children were 'too disturbed' to be seen, which influenced the solicitor's decision. Some of the children who were not seen by their solicitor expressed views that were different from those of their guardian. The small sample size of the study limits the conclusions that can be drawn from these findings. However, the study does suggest some cause for concern about the extent to which children and young people of this age group are actually involved in proceedings, what part the guardian and solicitor play in encouraging this involvement, and the way in which solicitors in particular represent them.

Masson and Winn Oakley's study, *Out of Hearing: Representing Children in Care Proceedings*, focuses on the way in which children and young people are represented in care proceedings by solicitors and guardians. It is based on the researchers' observations of meetings between 20 children and young people aged between 8 and 18 and their representatives, and on interviews with them after the proceedings had been concluded. Different aspects of the proceedings are considered and the perspectives of the professionals and the children and young people on these are discussed, examining for example the children's understanding of the roles of the two professionals; how guardians and solicitors interpreted their roles in relation to such things as representing the children's own views as to what should happen to them; the children's access to reports; and their attendance at the court hearing. Some graphic and detailed accounts are given about the experiences of individual children and the professionals' involvement. One account for example highlights the dilemmas of the guardian and solicitor over the retrieval of a skateboard on which one of the children had set his heart. The way in which the research findings are presented, interwoven as they are with longer discussions about, for example, policy and practice issues, lessens the book's usefulness as either a consumer study or an evaluation of the conduct of the professionals in the proceedings. Nonetheless, as the authors suggest, the focus on the point of view of children is innovative and goes some way to redressing its omission in other pieces of research.

Clark and Sinclair's study, *The Child in Focus: The Evolving Role of the Guardian* ad Litem, published in July 1999, examined the views of children aged over 8 years and guardians, social workers, solicitors and court personnel. The research was triggered by concerns about rising costs, in itself related to the increasing duration of care proceedings. It was based on 59 cases (from 30 London boroughs) completed in the first 6 months of 1998. All the cases were care proceedings. The authors endeavoured to ensure representativeness in the sample, given that the cases were drawn from two London GALRO Panels of unequal size (the Inner and North London Panel and the South London Panel).

The study provides detailed information, given that its broad aim was to achieve a wide perspective and its specific aims were firstly to describe the activities of guardians and relate them to the characteristics of cases and their costs; secondly to consider factors which contributed to effectiveness and added-value; and thirdly to consider the overall impact of guardians. In exploring the process as well as outcomes there were similarities with our own research study.

The views of eight children, aged between 7 and 13 years, were sought and the authors do comment that this was a smaller group than hoped. The children are reported to have spoken positively of their guardians and to be aware that the guardian was there for them, appreciating careful timing of interviews and unhurried discussion, but there was some confusion about the distinction between guardians and social workers. Feeling listened to and therefore given a part in the decision-making was valued.

Clark and Sinclair concluded that while the individual children benefited from the contribution of all parties, the specific value that was added by guardians was the representation of children's wishes and feelings, their skills in negotiating and mediating between various personnel, and their contribution to contact arrangements and to care plans. Indeed, they comment that it was in the detail of the care plan that guardians had most influence: 'The guardian's efforts to make sure care plans were both comprehensive and specific before the final hearing were part of the process of promoting the welfare of the child and keeping the child in focus throughout the proceedings' (p. 112).

One further study by Maria Ruegger on children's perspective of the

GALRO service has recently been completed but not yet published. This study involves 32 children, the largest sample to date.

Research reflecting children's views of their representatives is still in its infancy, but it is to be hoped that the current study, taken together with the four studies referred to here, will enable children and young people to contribute more effectively than hitherto to the development of the service, emphasising the need to take children's views into account and to learn from their feedback.

## CHILDREN'S VIEWS

Over recent decades there has been a change in the way children are perceived and a growing recognition that children should have a voice in matters that affect their lives. The 1989 Children Act, the 1995 Children (Scotland) Act and the United Nations Convention on the Rights of the Child have encouraged this reconceptualisation.

The UK Government ratified the United Nations Convention on the Rights of the Child on 16 December 1991. Article 12 is seen as the lynchpin of the Convention and states that children have the right to express their views and to have their views listened to and recognised as legitimate. The 1989 Children Act 'incorporates measures which seek to empower children ...' (Timms, 1995). The Act requires local authorities and courts to listen to children and involve them in decisions about the provision of welfare services, where they have sufficient understanding. It seems fitting that children influence the development of the guardian *ad litem* service because it is consistent with the central task of a guardian: to listen to children and represent their wishes and feelings in court.

Most research to date on childhood has used adults as proxies for children. Research in which both adults (usually parents) and children have provided accounts of children's lives have found consistent differences in the two accounts (Beresford, 1997). These findings demonstrate that adults cannot assume that they necessarily know what children are experiencing and feeling. Accounts such as these, and the reconceptualisation of children as 'active social agents' (Beresford, 1997), have influenced the way in which research with children has developed. Increasingly researchers are speaking to children directly in order to ascertain their experiences and views, a trend that is reflected in the recent surge in research with children on the guardian service.

Child-focused research presents researchers with a number of unique methodological and ethical issues that relate to the power imbalance between adult researchers and child participants. However, to date there have been surprisingly few written discussions on the practicalities and ethics of conducting research with children. Alderson's (1995) book, *Listening to Children: Children, Ethics and Social Research*, provides a rare guide for researchers on the ethics of social research with children and was particularly helpful in the design stage of the present research, enabling us to keep to the fore the ethical implications of our research methodology decisions. Alderson provides sound practical advice and guidelines and suggests ways of resolving dilemmas such as how to manage situations where it is necessary to breach confidentiality.

There is an increasing tendency for researchers to describe their experiences of the research process in papers separate from their research findings, highlighting methodological and ethical dilemmas and describing how these issues were resolved. Mauthner (1997), Mahon *et al.* (1996) and Hood *et al.* (1996) are three examples of such accounts.

Mauthner (1997) examined methodological issues raised in three studies carried out in home and school settings with children aged between two and 18 years and their parents. The emphasis was on methods that had been particularly successful at encouraging children to talk to researchers about a chosen topic. Individual interviews were found to be useful with children over 6 years of age. The studies raised the importance of tailoring the language used in interviews to suit a child's level of understanding. In one study separate interview schedules were produced for young people over 11 years of age and children younger than 10 years. Structured activities such as drawing, reading, playing games and sorting cards were used in one project and were found to help young children focus on the research topic of healthy eating.

Mahon *et al.* (1996) reflected on their experiences of conducting two research studies involving semi-structured interviews with children aged 9 to 17 years. They observed that one-to-one interviews were an appropriate method with older children and less successful, 'in terms of the depth of response and rapport established' (p. 149) with younger children. They suggest that different research methods might need to be used with younger children. They cited the 'write and draw' technique as a possible suitable method, further supporting the use of structured activities suggested by Mauthner (1997). The main concerns for Mahon *et al.* (1996) arising from their two studies related to confidentiality and disclosure. They shared the view that 'confidentiality can never be guaranteed to children because the researcher has a duty to pass on information to the appropriate professionals' (p. 151). The two studies reflected different approaches to addressing the issue of confidentiality. In one study confidentiality was guaranteed with the provision that if a child disclosed that someone in the family was at risk, the interviewer might inform a third party, in consultation with the child. In the second study total confidentiality was provisionally guaranteed with renegotiations taking place should a child's responses cause concern.

We have drawn on the suggestions in these accounts of how to engage with children ethically and successfully in designing our current study. In turn in this report we describe our experiences in conducting research with children in order to add to the collective practice wisdom of other researchers and to the development of good research practice in working with children.

Obtaining children's views of guardians provides only one part of the picture of the guardian service. In order to evaluate the whole of the guardian's practice it is necessary to obtain feedback from all parties involved in public family law proceedings; this includes social workers, solicitors, the court and the consumers of the guardian service (parents and children). The following two pieces of research go some way to addressing the views not only of children but also of some professionals; however, the views of carers including birth parents and foster carers and the court are still missing. It remains for other researchers to obtain these views.

## RESEARCH AIMS

The overall aim of this research was to broaden our limited understanding of how the guardian *ad litem* service is actually operating today, as seen from the perspective of some of the parties involved in public family law proceedings. To achieve this we undertook two separate studies with specific aims.

The aim of the research on professional's views was to explore what contribution guardians make throughout the course of proceedings and on the outcome. We wanted to establish whether the guardian's role was seen to be effective or particularly valued from the perspective of professionals involved in proceedings. Through this research we also sought to examine the processes in the working relationship of guardians and children's solicitors and the extent to which the roles of these two professionals overlap.

The aim of the research on children's views was to establish children's understanding of the guardian service and court process using a non-abusive research framework. We wanted to examine children's perspectives on the role of guardians in proceedings. Again we sought to explore children's views of their solicitors' role, since the guardian and children's solicitor work in partnership, with the shared responsibility of representing children.

In achieving these aims we hoped to facilitate a shift in the evaluation of guardian *ad litem* work from the final outcome to the process of decision-making.

By the time the research was completed a change in circumstances – the proposed development of the new Children and Family Court Advisory Service – had given it a new relevance not envisaged at its inception.

## OUTLINE OF THE REPORT

In Chapters 2 and 3 we describe the methodology and sample profile of the research concerning professionals' views, and examine professionals' perceptions of the guardians' relationships with other professionals and their contribution to a case. In Chapter 4 we look at the methodology of the children's research, and the profile of the children interviewed for the research. In Chapter 5 we explore children's perceptions of their guardian. In Chapter 6 we move on to examine children's experience of the court process, while in Chapter 7 we look at the legal representation of children. In Chapter 8 we compare and contrast children's and professionals' perceptions of the guardian *ad litem* service, and finally in Chapter 9 we explore the practice and policy issues arising from the study and their implications for the future.

Throughout this report guardians *ad litem* will be referred to more simply either as 'guardians' or 'GALs'. 'Children' will be used to denote both children and young people so as not to overload the text. 'Young people' or 'young person' will be used when specifically referring to adolescents. 'She', 'her' and 'herself' are used when children and young people are referring to their guardians and solicitors in order to preserve the anonymity of the children in these cases (there are more female guardians than male).

# CHAPTER 2

# The views of professionals: agreements and disagreements

## INTRODUCTION

Our intention in undertaking this study, as we indicated in the introduction, was to facilitate a shift in the evaluation of guardian work from the final outcome to the process of decision-making, that is, a focus on the 'means' rather than the 'end'. We hoped to establish whether or not it was true, as anecdotal evidence suggested, that although the final recommendations in a majority of cases were agreed by the professionals concerned, this agreement frequently disguised the negotiations concerning the detail of the recommendations that had occurred along the way and the extent to which the guardian had contributed to these. One of the aims of the study therefore was to evaluate what the professionals involved in the proceedings perceive to be the contribution made by guardians to public family law proceedings. We did this by exploring the views of the guardians, local authority social workers and the children's, parents' and local authority legal representatives who were involved in 21 cases of care proceedings completed by the Humberside GALRO Panel between 1 September 1997 and 23 January 1998.

The 21 cases randomly selected for inclusion in the study related to the work of 14 guardians from the Humberside GALRO Panel. Of the 14 guardians involved ten guardians had one case, two guardians had two cases, one guardian had three cases, and one guardian had four cases. The cases involved 36 children in all (i.e. the cases include a number of sibling groups) with an age range of 2 months to 16 years (see Table 1 below). Twelve cases involved multiple proceedings. We found the sample is typical of the range of applications for cases coming into the panel.

*Table 1* *Order sought for selected cases in professionals' research*

| Application | Number of cases | Ages of children* |
|---|---|---|
| Care | 4 | 16;1, 11;4, 11;4, 9;4, 1;0, 0;5 |
| Care and contact | 2 | 6;11, 4;8, 0;6 |
| Care and refuse contact | 1 | 0;9 |
| Care and residence | 3 | 15;4, 10;4, 9;1, 8;1, 4;10, 4;7, 3;11, 2;8 |
| Care and secure accommodation | 2 | 16;1, 15;4 |
| Care and freeing | 1 | 0;2 |
| Interim care | 2 | 7;10, 6;9, 3;7, 3;3, 1;2 |
| Discharge care and contact | 1 | 16;0, 14;3, 12;4, 7;7 |
| Contact | 1 | 4;1 |
| Contact, residence and supervision | 1 | 12;10, 8;6 |
| Discharge care and residence | 1 | 15;7 |
| Secure accommodation | 2 | 13;4, 12;10 |
| **Total** | **21** | |

*Years; months

A comparison of the sample and GALRO Panel by local authority can be found in Appendix 1.

## METHODOLOGY

Local authority solicitors, social workers, children's solicitors, parents' solicitors and guardians involved in 21 randomly selected cases were asked to complete a questionnaire, seeking their view of the guardian's role in a range of aspects of care proceedings. Twenty social workers, 14 local authority solicitors, 13 children's solicitors, 17 parents' solicitors and 18 guardians returned the questionnaire.

There were two versions of the questionnaire, one for guardians and one for non-guardians. The two questionnaires were identical but for 'you' being substituted for 'GAL' and the omission of the question 'How much "value added" has the GAL contributed to this case?' from the guardian questionnaire.

A total of 111 questionnaires were distributed to professionals. Eighty-two questionnaires were returned, giving an overall response rate of 73.8%. This high return rate would suggest that respondents valued the research and its aim of highlighting the contribution made by guardians to care proceedings. Social workers returned an impressive 95.2% of the questionnaires sent to them, local authority solicitors returned 66.6%, children's solicitors 61.9%, parents' solicitors 62.9% and guardians 85.7%.

Questionnaire data have been analysed through a combination of quantifying numerical incidence and detailed analysis of individual responses. In reporting the findings we shall focus upon the comments made by respondents. No attempt has been made in analysing the findings to consider whether or not there was consistency among the professionals in their comments on a particular case. This would not have been relevant in all the cases and, in any case, our main concern was to gain a sense of the professionals' perspective on the work of the guardians, rather than to establish a consensus about their contribution in a particular case.

## THE PROCESS OF DECISION-MAKING

We wanted to establish the number of cases in which the final recommendation to the court concerning the type of order sought was agreed by all the professionals concerned. We also wanted to find out whether or not there had been disagreements along the way, for example over the details of the care plan or management of the process of the proceedings, and the extent to which the guardian was seen by the other professionals as having had an influence on the way these issues were resolved. In discussing the findings, therefore, we consider first the numbers of cases where the final recommendation was the same. We then explore areas of agreement and disagreement. Next we consider the perceptions of the other professionals involved concerning the impact of the guardians' involvement, including the kinds of issues that the guardians introduced for consideration. Finally we consider more impressionistic reflections by the other professionals and the guardians themselves on the guardian's role.

In answer to the question 'Were the recommendations of the guardian in line with the local authority?', 74 (90.2%) indicated that they were and 8 (9.8%) replied that they were not. Since the latter related to two out of the 21 cases, it will be seen that a substantial majority reported agreement, which is consistent with the national profile.

Although in general guardians and the local authority agree in their final recommendations, their comments reveal areas of disagreement along the way; we shall explore these in more detail later. For example:

*Local authority took decision to initiate proceedings ... GAL
supported this application – lots of consultation took place around
issues of contact etc.*                                    (Social worker)

*The GAL too made useful suggestions about contact to father. The
GAL's input swayed the local authority's approach to be more child
centred.*                                               (Parent's solicitor)

*Initial care plan not endorsed until it was modified by negotiation.*
                                                        (Children's solicitor)

*Regarding the secure accommodation application ... I* [GAL]
*disagreed with lengths of order and Court followed my suggestion.*
                                                                 (GAL)

Eight professionals reported disagreement as to the final recommendation. These related to two of the 21 cases studied. In one of these cases, for example:

*The local authority did not favour any form of contact between father
and child at the outset.*                               (Mother's solicitor)

The guardian disagreed, and:

*A compromise was reached by negotiation* [for the] *local authority to
supervise father who violated terms of the agreement.*
                                                           (Social worker)

The guardian's recommendations were based upon

*Father's perceived commitment. Need for father to have a role. To
maintain a link for the future.*                        (Mother's solicitor)

The social worker reported that the

*Local authority did not disagree that* [the] *child required information
about her father but questioned the timing and the motivations for
father's wish for parental responsibility and contact.*

The comments above provide some indication that the final agreement between guardians and the local authority is arrived at through a process of assessment, discussion and negotiation during the course of proceedings. We now explore aspects of these negotiations; to identify the extent to which discussions took place and the issues that were discussed.

# THE CARE PLAN

## LOCAL AUTHORITY AND GUARDIAN AGREEMENT IN CARE PLAN RECOMMENDATIONS

In 16 of the 21 cases, the guardian, social worker and local authority solicitor reported that they were in agreement over recommendations made in the care plan. This result may suggest that, in the main, local authority care plans are appropriate to children's needs and are in their best interests, in the sense, that is, that the guardians endorsed the local authority recommendations. However, realistically for some cases the guardian and local authority may have agreed to a care plan that was achievable with the resources available to the local authority.

In five cases, professionals indicated disagreement between the local authority and GAL in their recommendations for the care plan. Comments relating to these cases are shown in Box 1 below.

---

**Box 1  Comments on differences in care plan recommendations between the local authority and GAL**

- Local authority had their hands tied by the health authority's refusal to give a mental illness diagnosis on this young person.

(GAL)

- [GAL] required it [care plan] to be more specific with clearer commitment and timescales. (Children's solicitor)

- Possible separation of siblings – GAL concerned and recommended psychologist assessment of this issue if to be put into practice. (Social worker)

- Difficulties in formulating a care plan and ensuring that the care plan would show [young person's] flexible needs. (GAL)

- At the final hearing the local authority produced a care plan which was in the children's best interest and therefore I [GAL] was in agreement during the final stages of proceedings with the local authority. (GAL)

- The local authority and the GAL differed about contact but after all party negotiations, agreement was arrived at. (Father's solicitor)

- GAL strongly criticised local authority rehabilitation plan to mother. (Social worker)

---

Specific areas of disagreement between the local authority and guardians are explored further later.

We also wanted to see, by looking at social workers' perception of the involvement of the guardians in the process, the extent to which they felt the guardians had contributed to the care plan. The Arrangements for Placement of Children Regulations place a statutory duty on authorities to write a care plan for a child whom they are proposing to look after. Generally it is the social worker's responsibility to write the care plan. The social worker must formulate the care plan in consultation with the child, the child's parents and other important individuals or agencies in the child's life, including guardians *ad litem*. The social worker, then, is in the best position to comment on the extent to which guardians influence the formulation of the final care plan. The comments of the social workers in this study suggest that in their view guardians make a valuable contribution to the formulation of care plans. In one case, the social worker considered that the guardian had had very great influence on the care plan: in seven cases 'quite a lot' of influence, in eight cases 'a little' influence, and in four cases 'no influence'.

The comments of the social workers give a flavour of the way in which this influence occurred, or the reasons why it had been relatively marginal or had not affected the care plan. For example, in two cases where the guardian had had 'a little' influence they commented:

> The guardian influenced the care plan 'a little' by initiating the use of experts to conduct a psychological assessment 'whose report the local authority found helpful' and 'to direct contact needs in the present and long-term planning'.

Seven social workers reported that the guardian had 'quite a lot' of influence on the care plan. For example, one said the guardian had 'spent a great deal of time listening to the children and to the needs of their carers (i.e. Aunt and Uncle)'.

One social worker reported that the guardian had influenced the final care plan 'very much', commenting: 'The GAL was very helpful not especially because she agreed with the local authority but because she undertook a thorough appraisal of the situation in her independent capacity.'

In four cases the social workers involved indicated that the guardian had had no influence on the care plan. Comments relating to three of these cases indicated that the GAL had not influenced the care plan because the social worker had formulated a care plan that addressed the child or young person's needs. For example, the GAL in one case stated: '[social work] practice was of high standard and all the issues considered by me [GAL] had been given careful consideration by the local authority.' For the fourth case, the GAL did not influence the care plan as it had been drawn up before the GAL had been appointed (the Panel operated a waiting list for some months).

## OTHER PROFESSIONALS' PERCEPTIONS OF THE EXTENT TO WHICH THE GUARDIAN INFLUENCED THE CARE PLAN

Although it may be argued that the social workers were in the best position to estimate the contribution of the guardians in relation to the care plan, the views of the other professionals were also sought. Local authority solicitors, children's solicitors and parents' solicitors recognised that guardians are often involved in negotiations with social workers that can change the final care plan. The comments of other professionals reflected a shared view with social workers that guardians make a valuable contribution to care plans. For example, commenting that the guardian had had 'a little' influence, one parent's solicitor observed that:

> GAL assisted in keeping local authority's mind open to pursue assessments of parents and to investigate contact issues.

(Parent's solicitor)

Of the professionals who found that the guardian had had 'quite a lot' of influence, one local authority solicitor commented:

> The GAL commissioned a psychological report on the child, which outlined the 'ideal' placement for the child. The report was influential in obtaining resources from the health authority, which may not have been available to the local authority.

And in suggesting 'very much' influence, a guardian commented:

> Care plan was changed not to separate children. (GAL)

The comments above reveal that social workers and guardians often work closely together towards formulating a comprehensive care plan. In some cases guardians had a greater knowledge of families than social workers because of their previous involvement. Guardians were able to assist social workers by providing information on the needs of children and their carers. In some cases guardians assisted social workers by initiating expert assessments. Overall, it appears that social workers value the contribution of guardians when drawing up a care plan, and that the other professionals, too, acknowledge their contribution.

## OTHER SPECIFIC AREAS OF DISAGREEMENT BETWEEN GUARDIAN AND LOCAL AUTHORITY

The intention of the following series of questions was to identify specific areas of disagreement between guardians and the local authority. These areas of potential disagreement range from issues to do with the process and management of the proceedings, such as timetabling and inter-agency co-operation, to specific details of the care plan, such as crucial arrangements over contact. Out of 82 professionals who responded a relatively small number of disagreements were reported in respect of individual cases. This result may indicate that the local authority and guardians have a good working relationship where disagreements are minimised through regular lengthy discussion. The low number of reported disagreements may also be partly accounted for by the likelihood that some professionals, particularly parents' solicitors, would be unaware of all discussions and disagreements that had occurred between social workers, local authority solicitors and guardians. More weight therefore may be given to the comments of these professionals. Comments related to five specific areas of disagreement, as described below.

### DISAGREEMENTS BETWEEN GUARDIAN AND LOCAL AUTHORITY OVER PROCEDURE

Ten professionals identified five cases in which the GAL and local authority disagreed during the proceedings over procedure. Comments revealed that disagreements were over expert assessments and a lack of liaison between social services departments.

*Expert assessments*
Four cases involved disagreements over expert assessments, for example:

> Couldn't pin the local authority down to obtaining proper expert evidence so had to do it ourselves.          (Children's solicitor)

*Liaison between social services departments*
One case involved a disagreement over the lack of liaison between social services departments. The local authority solicitor stated that 'the GAL

was very concerned about the lack of liaison with [another local authority that was involved].'

Six professionals identified five cases in which the local authority and guardian disagreed over the timetabling of proceedings. Only one of these cases had more than one professional reporting a problem over timetabling. This finding may indicate that the majority of professionals perceive difficulties over timetabling to be routine and not worthy of comment. Those who did consider the matter to be noteworthy provided comments such as the following:

> The GAL wished to accelerate the timetable as soon as it became clear that parents had returned to drug taking.    (Parent's solicitor)

> 'The local authority seemed content to let mother dictate the timetable. The GAL/legal advisor were very concerned to ensure the case received appropriate timetabling.    (Children's solicitor)

> There were huge delays when [the] young person was in secure when nothing positive was being done to get on with assessment.
> (GAL)

The comments indicate that when disagreements arise between the local authority and guardian over timetabling, they invariably relate to delays by the local authority, as perceived by guardians.

Thirteen professionals involved in six cases identified disagreements between the local authority and guardian over contact. Comments from these professionals revealed that disagreements concerned the timing of contact, the amount of contact between parents and their children, and the terms of contact.

*Timing of contact*

In two cases the guardian disagreed with the 'local authority taking the children out of school for contact sessions' (children's solicitor). This was particularly pertinent in one case in which the guardian reported that 'the children had learning needs ... and needed to miss no time from school'.

*Amount of contact*

Disagreements over the amount of contact between parents and their children were reported in two cases. In one case the social worker reported that disagreements over the 'level of contact the local authority wanted to provide to mother' were 'resolved as she withdrew completely from the case'. The social worker in the second case stated: 'Local authority felt a reduction in youngest child's contact to both parents may have been appropriate given her reluctance to attend. Prior to final hearing, local authority agreed to maintain existing arrangements – child [7-year-old] is capable of expressing wishes if not willing to attend.'

*The terms of contact*

One case involved disagreements over the terms of contact. The children's solicitor revealed that 'The local authority were not firm about contact, the GAL and carers were'.

## DISAGREEMENTS BETWEEN GUARDIAN AND LOCAL AUTHORITY OVER THINGS DONE/NOT DONE

Twenty-eight professionals involved in 14 cases identified that the guardian had disagreed with the local authority over things that they had or had not done. Areas of disagreement included the management of cases, inappropriate delays and placements, and the need for more assessments and financial support from the local authority. In relation to the management of cases, for example, a parent's solicitor commented:

*Local authority case very badly prepared and GAL insisted on adjourning final hearing ... to prevent collapse of local authority case, e.g. social worker unaware of experts' report and not contacted school for update.*

A guardian commented:

*The case had been badly managed at the outset. Relationship between social worker and family had broken down. There was no trust on either side.*

In relation to inappropriate delay:

*GAL concerned that local authority had not brought this case before court at an earlier time.*                                    (Social worker)

In the same case, the guardian commented that:

*When they did, it was a thorough, fully assessed decision.*

Other comments included concerns about inappropriate placements, the need for further assessments and further financial resources:

*The GAL was of the opinion that the local authority should have identified a move on placement earlier.* (Social worker)

*GAL required more comprehensive assessment work* [from local authority]. (Children's solicitor)

*GAL ... voiced concern that local authority management needed to fully financially support placement in order that more space/mobility could be afforded the family.* (Social worker)

## DISAGREEMENTS BETWEEN GUARDIAN AND LOCAL AUTHORITY OVER LEVEL OF COURT

There was only one reported disagreement between the local authority and guardian over choice of venue, cited by the children's solicitor. The guardian was opposed to a final hearing at a Family Proceedings Court as:

*This case had 14 potential witnesses. If any aspect was opposed it would not have been capable of being dealt with by* [court name] *FPC. The Court risked it and luckily mother gave up at last minute. If she hadn't there would have been substantial delay.*

This result indicates that, in general, the local authority and guardian agree over the level of court for proceedings. (The Family Proceedings Courts make the final decision of whether or not to transfer a case up when disagreements arise between local authority and guardian.)

## LOCAL AUTHORITY CONCERN OVER THINGS NOT DONE BY A GUARDIAN

It is also important to note that one social worker indicated concern over things a guardian had not done during a case. The social worker stated that the guardian: 'Did not consult with children in the family ... Did not consult with probation officer. Paid all attention to foster carer. Did not consult with other professionals or assessment officers'. This instance is of concern as, if accurate, it would seem that the guardian was not performing duties that are intrinsic to the role, especially as the case involved an application made by the father of a 4-year-old child for contact. It is not clear whether the social worker had drawn the guardian's attention to her/his concerns and, if so and not satisfied with the response, had then sought the advice of the Panel Manager regarding the use of either informal or formal complaints procedures.

CONCLUSION (SPECIFIC AREAS OF DISAGREEMENT)

From the above, we can see that where areas of disagreement between guardians and social workers were identified, these concerned issues of social work practice rather than issues arising specifically out of the court proceedings. They included:

- inappropriate placement of children and young people;
- delay or refusal to undertake assessment work by the local authority;
- inappropriate timing of contact sessions during school hours;
- hostile relationships between social workers and families.

The comments suggest that the guardian has a significant role to play in identifying and resolving issues, again reflecting that agreement over outcomes does not necessarily correlate with agreements during the process. These findings confirm the widely held belief that final agreement disguises the negotiations during the course of proceedings.

## DIFFERENCES BETWEEN ORDER SOUGHT AND ORDER GRANTED IN COURT

Professionals involved in six cases identified that the order granted in court was different to the original order sought. For 15 cases, the order sought was the same as the order granted in court.

Of the six cases, in two the parent withdrew her/his application after seeing the guardian's report.

The mother in one case withdrew her application for discharge contact and residence orders 'in the face of strong evidence against her case' (children's solicitor). The guardian of this case reported that 'Consistency amongst all the professionals made the success of mother's application most unlikely'.

In a further two the local authority changed their recommendations after seeing the expert's assessment. In one case, 'Care orders were sought in respect of older child and younger child' (local authority solicitor). 'The department took heed of the assessments completed by psychiatrist, independent social worker and psychologist' (social worker). As such, 'A care order was made in regard of older child only' (local authority solicitor).

In the fifth case, the change between order sought and order granted was a result of a 'positive change in the parents assisted by a comprehensive assessment schedule including significant family support and increased co-operation from family' (social worker). The local authority changed its recommendation 'during the course of proceedings from a care order to a supervision order' (local authority solicitor).

Finally, in the sixth case, the circumstances were such that a compromise was reached. The father had 'applied for actual direct contact with the child that was never feasible' (parent's solicitor). The local authority drew up a compromise agreement with father for 'an indirect contact order providing for work to be done with mother, father and children to allow the situation to move on' (parent's solicitor).

In none of these cases was it the court that finally arbitrated, i.e. the orders were made with consensus.

## CONTRIBUTION OF THE GUARDIAN TO AGREEMENT

We were interested in seeing the extent to which the social workers and other professionals considered that the GAL had contributed to the case being agreed, since clearly this is significant in terms of assessing the guardians' contribution to the process of the case, which may not be apparent in the final outcome. In ten cases, the social workers perceived that the GAL had contributed significantly ('very much') to the case being agreed; in four cases 'quite a lot'; in three cases 'a little'; in two cases 'not at all'; and in one case it was not applicable.

In the cases where the guardians were seen as contributing significantly, the social workers commented, for example:

*GAL saw both parents together and separately and transmitted, very clearly, her views regarding protection of the child.*

*Local authority had strong evidence that neither parent had significantly changed and thus increased unsupervised contact ... was not appropriate. GAL agreed ... I [social worker] feel her views lent strength to parents withdrawing their applications.*

And in the cases where the guardian was seen as having 'quite a lot' or 'a little' influence, comments included:

*Birth father already in agreement with the local authority but additional insight of the GAL of assistance.*

*Possible separation of sisters – GAL concerned and recommended psychological assessment ... if to be put into practice i.e. before a decision made. More detailed statement put to court to explain reasoning behind plan. Separation not being acted on.*

The social worker in two cases indicated that the guardian had made no contribution to the case being agreed, commenting for example:

*This case is not a good example of a GAL being involved to any great extent due to the history of recent care proceedings on previous three children.*

Overall, then, social workers reported that guardians made some contribution, often substantial, to the fact that 17 cases were uncontested at the end of proceedings. This contribution came from their involvement with parents and the local authority, and in commissioning expert assessments throughout the course of the proceedings. Local authority solicitors, children's solicitors, guardians and parents' solicitors also identified that guardians made a marked contribution towards cases being non-contested. The views of some of these professionals will now be examined.

The guardians, too, considered that they had contributed to the case being agreed, and although they differed slightly from the perceptions of the social workers (considering, for example, that they had contributed 'very much' to the case being agreed in two cases rather than ten, and 'quite a lot' in seven as opposed to the four cited by the social workers), in general they considered that they had made some clear contribution. For example, two guardians (out of the five who reported having contributed 'a little') commented:

*Mother, father, grandmother and aunt all agreed with care order ... and their views did not change after I saw them.*

*Assisted in helping the mother to consider the needs of the children and to accept that they were receiving good quality care in the placement.*

Similar to the comments of social workers, guardians who reported that they had contributed 'quite a lot' or 'very much' indicated that their contribution was made through their involvement with parents and the local authority, for example:

*I spent a great deal of time working with the parents. I think the social worker had a difficult relationship with them.*

*Father, who had been frustrated by SSD [Social Services*

Department] *actions, refused to have anything to do with social worker. I did a lot of liaison, observation of contact etc.*

We also looked at the extent to which the solicitors involved considered that the guardians contributed towards a case being agreed. Four children's solicitors and one local authority solicitor reported that the guardian had contributed 'very much' towards their case being non-contested. The children's solicitor and local authority solicitor in one case, for example, suggested that the guardian had contributed a great deal by taking 'time to speak to the [13-year-old young person] and explain the position regarding consent and the manner in which proceedings would be dealt with' (local authority solicitor). The remaining children's solicitor reported that the case was 'Only agreed as a result of round the table discussions on day of final hearing at which guardian had significant contribution'.

In two other cases, the guardian's contribution was seen to have been through her/his work with a teenage client:

*By giving clear and unequivocal advice to teenage client regarding poor prospects of defending* [secure accommodation] *application, such advice being accepted leading to instructions to agree.*

*The GAL explained and discussed matters with young person in such a way as to ensure she fully understood what was happening and the consequences.*

One children's solicitor and seven local authority solicitors reported that the guardian had 'a little' influence on their case being uncontested. In commenting on the reason for this low level of involvement, one children's solicitor commented: 'This was effectively an uncontested case, the parents did not attend the proceedings, file evidence or co-operate'.

## WHETHER THE CONCERNS OF THE GUARDIAN WERE THE SAME AS THOSE OF THE LOCAL AUTHORITY

Professionals revealed few differences in the concerns of the guardian and local authority during the course of proceedings. One social worker, two parents' solicitors and three children's solicitors indicated that the guardian and local authority differed markedly in their concerns. Interestingly, guardians and local authority solicitors did not consider that there was any marked difference in their concerns.

In the five cases where differences were noted the concerns were over children's needs versus parental needs, the suitability of a placement and the role of a father in one case. From these findings it appears that the guardian and local authority had similar concerns in a majority of cases, suggesting good liaison between the guardian and local authority throughout the course of proceedings.

Professionals identified a range of concerns that were shared by the local authority and guardian, including drug use by young people, the behaviour of parents and the risk posed by Schedule One offenders (people with convictions for offences against children, under Schedule One of the 1933 Children Act). For example:

*Social worker and myself ... were concerned for child's health and were anxious to mover her on in terms of her use of drugs.*

*Concerns were the same although I felt rehabilitation needed to be kept in mind at all times.*

Relatively few comments discussed how concerns had come to be shared by the guardian and local authority, but from a few comments it seems that agreement was reached through discussions between the local authority and guardian in which information was shared with mutual respect shown by both parties. It seems likely, too, that meetings between the GAL and local authority throughout the course of proceedings are helpful in moving cases along towards a speedier and satisfactory outcome.

## CONCLUSION

The comments presented above reveal that in most agreed cases guardians are seen by all the professionals concerned as contributing, often significantly, towards agreement. It seems likely that a guardian's independence allows her/him access to all parties and s/he can act as a mediator when there are 'sticking' points, for example on adjustments to care plans and disagreements between parents and the local authority. Guardians provide an unbiased and child-centred view to proceedings. Parents in particular respect this viewpoint. Parents also respond positively to guardians spending time listening to them and sharing investigation findings. Consequently the presence of guardians makes decision-making by parents and social workers easier. In some cases guardians are able to move parties towards agreement.

# CHAPTER 3

# Adding value: views on the guardian's contribution

## NEW INFORMATION AND ISSUES RAISED IN THE GUARDIAN *AD LITEM* INVESTIGATION

In 17 of the 21 cases one or more professionals involved reported that the guardian had raised new information or issues during the course of proceedings. All 32 professionals who identified that the guardian in their case had revealed new information or issues provided further detail of the guardian's role. We report these in some detail, since they clarify the contribution to proceedings on the part of the guardian, by identifying what types of new information and issues were raised, the consequence of these revelations and why the information and issues had not been raised previously (Table 2).

*Table 2* *Guardian's role in providing new information and issues in child care proceedings*

| New piece of information or issue | Reason for information or issue not being raised previously |
|---|---|
| ***Information on the views of parents*** | |
| • *GAL's vast knowledge of the case undoubtedly had a valuable input for the local authority* (Children's solicitor) | • *GAL was a constant, the social worker changed over time* (Children's solicitor) |
| • *Views of putative father* (Children's solicitor) | • *Lack of enthusiasm on part of local authority* (Children's solicitor) |
| • *General information GAL obtained from the parents regarding their views/ situation* (Local authority solicitor) | |

### Information on criminal history

- GAL was instrumental in obtaining information from Crown Court proceedings concerning father's offences and introducing them into Children's Act proceedings. Also, GAL liaised with father's former wife and daughter regarding history of offending (Parent's solicitor)

- The father had given misleading information about past relationships (Social worker)

- Social workers are not able to investigate because of work pressures (GAL)

### Information on medical evidence

- Identification of an aunt who could contribute to Life Storybook information. Provision of medical information (expert opinion on baby; information from mother's physician) which contributed to assessment and conclusions (GAL)

- The GAL commissioned an experts report so that there was clear evidence...that mother had taken heroin during her pregnancy (Parent's solicitor)

- The existence of the aunt had been lost to SSD because of changes of social workers. Also, the SSD did not seek to interview relatives as I did ... I informed SSD that I would seek medical information (GAL)

- The LA medical evidence was not convincing on this point (Parent's solicitor)

- The experts report obtained by GAL identified by psychologist and psychiatrist problems not previously identified (Parent's solicitor)

- The social worker fell at the first hurdle when they could not get the child a psychiatrist to make a diagnosis of mental illness (GAL)

- The appointment of psychologist put serious doubt on young person's evidence but also found possible emotional abuse. Also, GAL had different relationship to local authority with young person (Children's solicitor)

- There was only evidence of emotional harm following the GAL's referral for a psychological assessment by psychologist (GAL)

### Issue of the potential role of extended family

- Identified possible carers within natural family (Children's solicitor)

- Local authority had failed to properly balance the attachment of children to family members ... against risks posed by the

> father, which may have been
> manageable (Children's solicitor)

- *Extended family structures, especially the viability of grandparents as carers* (Children's solicitor)

- *Local authority funds* (Children's solicitor)

## Issue of the situation of family members

- *Firstly, my* [GAL] *interview with natural father and his family revealed him to be far more concerned and helpful than local authority statements. Secondly, my interview with mother also suggested need for further family work* (GAL)

- *Because the nature of social work, information gathering is not comprehensive and the crises which precipitated the legal* [secure accommodation] *proceedings did not give much opportunity for calm meetings with family* (Social worker)

- *One father's supervised contact had been summarily stopped on grounds that he was not keeping appointments. In fact SSD had stopped contact due to lack of staff* (GAL)

- *SSD did not realise what had happened until I looked through SSD and Family Centre records ... Made little difference to father's perception of SSD – refused to engage with them* (GAL)

- *Concerns regarding relative carer and impact of the family conflict upon the child's placement* (GAL)

- *The family member who shared information regarding relative carer not having driving licence etc. did not share information with SSD ... did not trust SSD* (GAL)

- *Identified stresses and strains in the carers* (Social worker)

- *GAL was first on the scene and kept herself very much up to date* (Social worker)

## Issue of the use of experts

- *In respect of making more use of psychologist who was working with the children for more profound assessments of the children's wishes and feelings and needs in respect of short-term and long-term contact* (GAL)

- *The young age of some of the children ... and consequent assumptions of what could be understood from, and by, them* (GAL)

### Issue of the appropriateness of care plan recommendations

- *The GAL seriously questioned the rehabilitation of the child back with mother* (Parent's solicitor)

- *Apathy, resources* (Children's solicitor)

- *Adoption as opposed to long-term foster care* (Children's solicitor)

### Issue of specialist work for children

- *Need for further individual work to be done with one of the children. As the social worker involved for 3 years it was helpful to have a fresh pair of eyes* (Social worker)
- *I [GAL] suggested that background checks in respect of mother's new husband be done ... as little was known about him. This was done* (GAL)

- *Firstly, the foster carer ... had undertaken the task and had made some progress. The social worker acknowledged that specialist work might be more appropriate. Secondly, ... all contact with the family ... is supervised by local authority staff* (GAL)

From these comments it appears that during the course of some proceedings guardians are in a unique position to identify new information and bring new issues to the attention of other professionals. Respondents revealed that guardians raise new information on the views of parents, the criminal history of parents and medical evidence. The guardians in the 17 cases shown above also addressed issues around the potential role and situation of extended family members, the use of experts to obtain the wishes and feelings of children, the inappropriateness of care plan recommendations, and the need for specialist work with children. In a majority of the cases, the professionals placed the responsibility for issues and information not being raised or addressed with social services departments. Professionals considered that issues and information were not raised because of:

- the distrustful relationship between social workers and families;
- changes in social workers appointed to cases;
- the inferiority of medical experts and evidence available to the local authority;
- lack of funds available to the local authority; and
- time constraints on social workers, prohibiting the conduct of a comprehensive investigation.

It is curious that no professional identified that the guardian raised new information about the children, or their views, as reflected in the children's research (see Chapters 5 and 6).

## WHETHER THE SAME OR A SIMILAR OUTCOME WOULD HAVE BEEN ACHIEVED WITHOUT A GUARDIAN

This question is, by its nature, speculative. However, it does address the impressions from anecdotal evidence that the guardian has considerable impact on the process itself as well as the decision-making. While the findings show that the impact of the guardian is less significant where the outcome was clear-cut and where social services input was of a high standard, it follows that the impact is likely to be greatest where issues are contested. The value placed on the guardian's contribution by other professionals may be gauged by inviting them to reflect on the likelihood of their being a different outcome had the guardian not been involved.

Twenty-six professionals reported that their case would have had a different outcome if a guardian had not been involved. Their comments relate to 15 out of 21 cases, and include such observations as:

*The court may have renewed the secure order and so young person may have been placed differently.*    (Social worker; no order made)

*The local authority would have continued trying to obtain a care order because of older child's allegations of sexual abuse when there was no evidence that this happened. The local authority seemed unwilling to question this.*    (GAL; no order made)

Comments indicated that some cases would have been longer without guardian involvement. For example:

*It would have taken years to resolve without a GAL. Also the role of the GAL was that of mediator in several situations.*    (GAL)

Professionals also commented that without a guardian some cases might have been contested:

*The parents may not have believed what the local authority said about the children's views and the matter may then have been contested.*    (Local authority solicitor)

*The parties were able to deal with the guardian as an independent person ... matters progressed with less conflict due to mother's confidence in GAL.*    (Parent's solicitor)

These comments suggest that the presence of a guardian not only affects the type of order made in some proceedings, but also how and when an order is reached. That is, guardians can influence whether an order is reached with agreement or conflict between parties and with or without delay. Comments made by professionals who believed that the same outcome would have been reached had there not been a guardian reported this also.

Forty-seven professionals reported that the same or a similar outcome would have been achieved if a guardian had not been appointed. Comments relating to these reports highlighted three reasons why this was the case:

- the outcome was 'clear-cut' and inevitable;
- social services input was of a high standard;
- GAL involvement was minimal.

Twelve professionals commented that the same or a similar outcome would have occurred without a guardian because the outcome was 'clear-cut', for example:

*This was an unusual case. In normal circumstances the GAL's view may be sought more actively and the contribution of the GAL is more important. The recent care proceedings had the most important bearing in this case.*                              (Social worker)

*A care order would have been made in any case.*
                                                    (Local authority solicitor)

The guardian and children's solicitor in one case reported that owing to the work of a highly skilled social worker the outcome would have been similar if a guardian had not been appointed. Their comments were:

*There was no realistic alternative to the care plan, and the social worker was dedicated and experienced.*        (Children's solicitor)

*The case was effectively managed. The social worker worked hard, reflected upon her actions, and she followed procedure. For these reasons this case would have had a similar outcome.*        (GAL)

In one case a local authority solicitor reported that the same outcome would have occurred without a guardian due to 'the lack of contribution by the GAL'.

One guardian reported that s/he was not involved at the beginning of proceedings, when 'Solicitor for the child was able to take instructions from child directly' and thus a care order was made without GAL involvement. However, 'at the first hearing for secure accommodation order the Magistrates said they had found my [GAL] contribution helpful in understanding the situation and what to do' (GAL).

Several professionals considered that the same outcome would have been achieved without a guardian but the proceedings would have been more contentious and longer, as the following comments illustrate:

*It would have been a most contentious case without the GAL.*
(Parent's solicitor)

*The GAL was a major factor in avoiding an adversarial/contentious approach.*    (Local authority solicitor)

*However, quite possibly not by agreement.*    (Social worker)

*However, I think that the process would have been more drawn out. That would not have been in the children's best interests.*    (GAL)

### Conclusion (same or similar outcome without a guardian)

Comments revealed that in some cases guardians contribute to changes between orders applied for and the type of order made. However, responses also demonstrate the qualitative effect of guardian involvement, which does not necessarily show in simple statistics, such as order applied for and order made. For example, the parents' acceptance of the need for an order or for the nature and quantity of contact will have far-reaching effects on the child after legal proceedings end.

Where the quality of the social worker's intervention is of a high standard, then the need for the contribution from the guardian is likely to be significantly reduced. Nevertheless, many of the comments illustrate the positive influence of guardians, which seems particularly to arise from their independent position so that the guardian's view adds weight to or confirms the social work view.

## VIEWS ON HOW MUCH VALUE THE GUARDIAN ADDED

It was thought not appropriate for guardians to answer the question 'How much value added has the guardian contributed to this case?'. This question therefore was put to all professionals other than guardians. The responses to this question suggest that although it might be criticised on the grounds that it is insufficiently clear, there exists a consensus as to its meaning with professionals providing similar ratings across cases. Comments provided across cases were also on similar themes. Some variations are to be expected, since professionals have different perspectives and levels of involvement with guardians.

Of the 64 non-guardians who returned a questionnaire, only two reported that the guardian had added no value to their case. Fourteen professionals reported that the guardian had added 'a little' value. Forty-seven professionals reported that the guardian had added 'quite a lot' or 'very much' value to their case, with one professional failing to answer the question. These figures indicate that, for the majority of professionals, guardians add considerable value to a case.

The two 'not at all' ratings relate to separate cases. One local authority solicitor reported that 'the guardian did a minimal amount of work in this case and had a very laid-back approach.' This is of concern, particularly since the case ran for nearly 11 months. Also of concern is the report by a social worker that the guardian's contribution to the case 'caused anxiety to the family, especially child on care order'. In this case, the guardian recommended that a contact order be made to the father who subsequently visited the child 'in a state of drunkenness', which in the view of the social worker 'badly frightened and traumatised' the child. Clearly there are issues here about the quality of practice, which will be discussed further in Chapter 9.

Comments provided by 14 professionals to ratings of 'a little' included the following:

> *For the young person whose liberty was restricted* [secure accommodation application] *it was important that an independent outsider maintained vigilance that her interest was served.*
>
> (Social worker)

> [Young person] *was most definitely in need of an independent person to be her representative and voice in this case.*
>
> (Local authority solicitor)

> *The guardian ... endeavoured to contact the parents and to evoke a response from them but with little success.*    (Children's solicitor)

> *The matter was a simple contact issue.*    (Parent's solicitor)

> *The social worker was committed and skilful.*    (Parent's solicitor)

From these comments it appears that guardians have only 'a little' value added in cases where the outcome is inevitable and social work practice is of a high standard. However, this 'little' value does not mean that the guardian is made redundant. The first two comments above highlight the importance of having an independent person to represent the wishes and feelings of the child or young person in order to safeguard her/his interests.

Out of 47 ratings of 'quite a lot' and 'very much', 13 were from social workers, 8 from local authority solicitors, 11 from children's solicitors and 15 from parent's solicitors. The reports related to 19 out of 21 cases. Comments provided revealed that the guardian's substantial contribution came from their ability to:

• express the wishes and feelings of children;
• provide an unbiased view of a case leading to final settlement;
• explain the court process to children;
• assist the local authority to focus upon salient issues; and
• provide a thorough investigation.

For example, in relation to expressing the wishes and feelings of children, two local authority solicitors commented:

*The guardian was able in conferences to add young person's views to the local authority's plans.*

*The views of the children were very important in this case and the guardian was the appropriate person to put those views before the court.*

In providing an unbiased view leading to settlement, a parent's solicitor commented:

*It would have been a most contentious case without the guardian and the ability of the family to work with local authority to help the child in care would have been jeopardised.*

In relation to explaining the court process to children, one children's solicitor commented:

*Children had no meaningful relationship with the social worker whatsoever and thus found it important to have their own guardian/solicitor.*

In helping the local authority to focus, one solicitor reported:

> Without the guardian things could have been a lot harder and
> possibly less constructive. The guardian's voice was a constructive
> one throughout which helped everyone involved focus on the salient
> issues at stake.                              (Local authority solicitor)

In relation to providing a thorough investigation, one parent's solicitor commented:

> Guardian's background knowledge of the case was crucial at the
> application for the interim care order which was contested.

## CONCLUSION (CONTRIBUTION OF GUARDIANS)

The comments presented above reveal the high regard of professionals for the work of most guardians. The substantial contribution made by guardians to proceedings arises from their position as independent people whose remit is to undertake a comprehensive investigation and express the wishes and feelings of children, keeping the focus on children throughout. In the process the guardian encourages the local authority to keep the salient issues to the fore. In many instances the guardian's involvement has facilitated settlement. Thus, the added presence of guardians can make some proceedings less contentious, shorter, more comprehensive and more child-focused. One can deduce that this is a better outcome for the children, not only because delay and contentious-ness can be prejudicial, but also because of the positive effect on present and future work with the children and their families.

## GENERAL COMMENTS

At the end of the questionnaire professionals were given an opportunity to provide 'further observations about the guardian in this case or in general'. Fifty-three professionals took up this opportunity. The comments covered a wide range of topics and generally praised the work of guardians and social workers.

Five professionals criticised the actions of a specific guardian, local authority or social worker. The comments included the following:

> This is generally not my view of guardians' contribution but in this
> instance the wishes and feelings of the children ... were not
> consulted ... guardian did not fully explore the extensive work
> and monitoring by the local authority and other agencies involved ...

*she had observed only one contact at my request and only saw*
*mother once.*                                    (Social worker)

*This guardian is not proactive or involved enough in the hands-on work*
*of the case. Her reports are articulate and theoretical. However, I fully*
*support the general role of the guardian.*    (Local authority solicitor)

*Very pleasant guardian but one who worked from instinct rather than*
*a clear knowledge base. This guardian would not inspire confidence*
*in a case where the issues were less clear-cut.*    (Social worker)

The remaining comments were positive towards guardians and the social services department. They included favourable comment on the way in which the guardian addresses the needs and interests of children; the competence and professionalism of guardians; their importance to proceedings; the high regard in which they are held by the courts; their extensive knowledge of families; the quality of social work practice; and the good working relationship that existed between guardians and social workers. For example:

*GAL worked with the department in a very professional way and did*
*not appear to 'take sides'.*                    (Social worker)

*Guardian very thorough and professional throughout. Down to earth*
*and accessible to children.*                    (Children's solicitor)

*In general the guardian's contribution is very important and can shed*
*a different light on a case which will normally assist the SSD.*
                                                (Social worker)

*Generally speaking the role of the guardian is extremely important to*
*the court proceeding as this presents a totally independent view.*
                                        (Local authority solicitor)

*The guardian plays a vital role. The views of the guardian are highly*
*regarded by the LA and by the court. All parties appreciate the*
*weight given to the views of the guardian by the court, and the*
*guardian is therefore in a unique position to resolve matters.*
                                                (Parent's solicitor)

*Guardian acted, as always, compassionately and fairly with all parties*
*and due to long involvement was able to assist the case towards the*
*right conclusion.*                             (Children's solicitor)

*The only negative point was, as in care proceedings, on the making*

*of the final order the guardian ceased to be involved. Given the
nature of the application* [secure accommodation] *it would have been
helpful if the guardian could have remained involved to oversee the
implementation of the support/work offered to the child.*

(Local authority solicitor)

*The guardian ... reported that she felt I* [social worker] *had done
everything I could to help mother parent her child. It was nice to
receive a letter from her after the court hearing commenting on the
good social work practice in this case. It's not often a social worker
receives praise!*                                    (Social worker)

*Throughout my career as a child care practitioner I have worked with
many guardians. I have found them to be generally helpful and
informative with good working relationships developed.*

(Social worker)

These more general comments from professionals shed a positive light
on the work of guardians and social workers. More importantly, this feedback summarises some of the reasons why the role of the guardian is
unique and vital to public family law proceedings.

## CONCLUSION

Overall, the findings support the hypothesis that the research was
designed to test: namely, that guardians contribute substantially to the
process of decision-making in care proceedings. Their contribution is
well regarded by other professionals. In particular, social workers, who
may be considered to be in the best position to assess this, value their
contribution highly. The findings also reveal that guardians *ad litem* contribute in a number of ways towards making proceedings less contentious, shorter, more comprehensive and more child-focused. These
findings highlight the importance of moving beyond an examination of
recommendations and final orders granted when evaluating the guardian
*ad litem* service.

In a majority of the 21 cases, the final recommendations were agreed
by all the professionals concerned, and this is consistent with the national
profile of agreed cases going before the courts. However, the responses to
the large majority of the questions indicate that the guardians are seen as
contributing, usually substantially, to the *process* of decision-making.
The respondents suggest in their comments that guardians contribute

significantly by identifying new information that needs to be considered in drawing up the care plan and by helping to make sure that the proceedings are conducted satisfactorily, for example by identifying the need for expert witnesses or by ensuring that a time framework is adhered to. Although in many instances it seems that the guardians' contribution comes from addressing deficiencies in the service provided by local authorities, they are also seen as valuable in providing an independent voice, which may be more acceptable to other parties, in particular birth families, to the proceedings. Many respondents recognised that arriving at agreements that were understood and accepted by all parties had an importance for the children concerned that went far beyond the immediate outcome of the court hearing.

Clearly, the guardian's contribution is more significant in some areas than it is in others. For example, many professionals considered that the outcome would have been the same, with or without the guardian's involvement. The findings, too, make no attempt to establish consistency between the professionals in their views of particular cases, and some of the questions, in particular those on value added and alternative outcomes, invite speculative and impressionistic responses from those involved. Nonetheless, taken as a whole, the findings suggest an overwhelming recognition of and positive support for the work of the guardians in care proceedings. The comments made by professionals provide a graphic account of the contribution made by guardians to care proceedings. They are, we would argue, more illuminating that a mere examination of statistics.

There is clearly a need for further research to provide evidence of the contribution made by both guardians and children's solicitors to public family law proceedings. Rather than a static and perhaps over-simplistic look at the correlation between orders sought and orders granted, it is hoped that future research will continue to focus on the process of decision-making during proceedings and the consequent benefits to children.

# The children's research methodology

In this chapter we will describe the research sample and methodology in some detail. We were determined that the children who participated should be from a representative sample, that there should be statistical validity, and that the process itself should be child-focused and non-abusing.

The research methods were developed to take into account cognitive and linguistic development and involved both games and drawings. (Figure 2 shows the board game that was developed.) A schedule was devised for the interview to enable a comparison of responses, while permitting some flexibility.

## SAMPLE SELECTION

The children were drawn from a potential group of 100 8- to 17-year-olds who were involved in public law proceedings between 1 June 1998 and 31 December 1998. Emergency protection order applications and proceedings under the Adoption Act were excluded. Some children were excluded at the request of adults (professionals or parents) for a variety of reasons ranging from the death of a parent to multiplicity of people already involved. The findings are based on the responses of 28 children aged between 8 years and 15 years.

The choice of a lower age limit of 8 years was made on the basis that by this age most children have sufficient linguistic skills to verbalise their opinions and are capable of recalling events in some detail. The age range of 8–17 years provided a potential sample of around 40% of the children represented by guardians from the Humberside Panel.

Seventeen children (17%) were excluded from the research on the advice of their guardian and social worker. Seventeen (17%) additional children were excluded from the research after initial contact with guardians owing to delays since the final hearing, new proceedings or lack of contact with their guardian.

A letter was sent to all those who had parental responsibility for the remaining 66 children. A leaflet explaining the nature and purpose of the research was included along with a letter addressed to the child. It was at the discretion of those living with the child as to whether s/he received the letter and leaflet, and/or were informed about the research. Children and their carers could return a slip or telephone the researcher to indicate that they wanted to arrange an interview or be excluded from the research.

The parents and/or carers of 18 children did not respond. Ten children declined to be in the research. The parents or carers of ten children replied that they did not want their children to be interviewed. Twenty-eight children agreed to participate and the research is based on their responses.

## PROFILE OF THE CHILDREN INTERVIEWED

Those who were interviewed were compared with those who were not in terms of gender, type of proceedings, local authority, person living with child (see Appendix 2), age and length of proceedings. No differences that would normally be regarded as statistically significant were found using chi-square and Kruskal–Wallis non-parametric tests.

The average age of the 28 children who were interviewed was 11.4 years (range 8.3–15.2). Eighteen (64%) children were aged between 8 and 11 years. There were 16 girls (57%) and 12 boys (43%) in the sample (see Fig. 1). This compares with Humberside GALRO Panel figures over the same 6-month period for 5- to 15-year-olds where there were 51% of girls and 49% of boys.

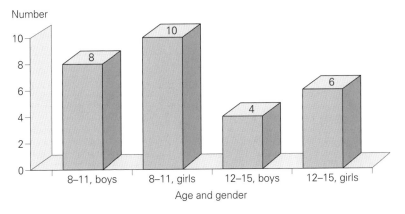

*Fig. 1* *Age and gender of children interviewed*

At the time of the interview, 11 children were living in foster care, six were living with their mother, two were living with their father, one child was living with both parents, four were in secure accommodation and four were living in a residential unit.

There were six sibling groups in the sample: five groups involved two siblings and there was one family of five children. The children interviewed came from 19 cases. Fourteen guardians were involved in these 19 cases, representing 43% of guardians on the Humberside GALRO Panel. Eleven guardians were involved in one case each, two guardians had two cases each, and one guardian was involved in four cases. Some guardians may have been over-represented in the sample because of their preference for working with older children.

*Table 3*  Number of children interviewed and related cases by type of proceeding

| Type of proceeding | Number of children interviewed N = 28 (%) | Number of cases* N = 19 (%) |
|---|---|---|
| Care | 17 (60.7%) | 10 (52.6%) |
| Care and contact | 3 (10.7%) | 2 (10.5%) |
| Care and residence | 1 (3.6%) | 1 (5.3%) |
| Discharge of care | 3 (10.7%) | 2 (10.5%) |
| Secure accommodation | 2 (7.1%) | 2 (10.5%) |
| Contact and residence | 1 (3.6%) | 1 (5.3%) |
| Supervision | 1 (3.6%) | 1 (5.3%) |

*A case is defined as a child or sibling group.

Seventeen (60.7%) children in the sample were involved in a care proceeding compared with 54% from the Humberside GALRO Panel. Three (10.7%) children in the sample were in a discharge of care proceeding compared with 7% from the Panel. Two (7.1%) children in the sample were in a secure accommodation proceeding compared with 2.4% from the Panel. One (3.6%) child was involved in a supervision case compared with 2% from the Panel (see Table 3).

Cases were open for a minimum of 28 days (secure accommodation) and a maximum of 421 days (care proceeding). The average length of cases involving the children interviewed was just over 6 months, that is 192 days.

***Table 4*** *Average duration of cases (in days) by type of proceeding for sample and Humberside Panel*

| Type of proceeding | Sample of children interviewed ($N = 28$) | Humberside GALRO Panel June 1998– December 1998 ($N = 206$) |
|---|---|---|
| Care | 273.7 | 282.9 |
| Contact | 283 | 266.1 |
| Discharge of care | 77 | 146.8 |
| Supervision | 146 | 218 |
| Secure accommodation | 31.5 | 38.8 |

The average length of cases involving the children interviewed appears to be similar to Humberside GALRO Panel figures for care, contact and secure accommodation proceedings. It appears that the durations of the discharge of care and supervision cases for the children interviewed were shorter than the average for the Panel (see Table 4).

A comparison of the sample and GALRO Panel by local authority can be found in Appendix 1.

## MEASURES

To address the aim of creating a non-abusive research framework, child-friendly research tools were devised. In creating the measures for this research we were aware that we had to address issues that affect interviews with both children and adults, such as the need to establish rapport, assure confidentiality and present questions clearly and consistently (Hill *et al.*, 1996). In addition, the research tools needed to match the children's level of cognitive and linguistic development and make use of materials and settings that were familiar to children (Garbarino *et al.*, 1992). The resulting four research tools, based on games and drawings, were in different formats to help engage and maintain children's interest in the interview. Our aim was to provide an enjoyable experience so that the children would leave the interview feeling good about their participation in the research.

### INTERVIEW SCHEDULE FOR CHILDREN

A semi-structured interview schedule was devised to be used with children who were over 11 years of age. Eight young people did the interview schedule, which consisted of 27 questions. The interview schedule was constructed to allow questions to be tailored to suit a child's cognitive and linguistic skills and personal experiences. It also allowed for a comparison of responses, without a loss of flexibility.

The interview schedule was divided into sections related to eight issues/events in chronological order:

(1) introduction to your guardian;
(2) understanding of the guardian's role;
(3) visits by your guardian;
(4) how you got along with your guardian;
(5) the guardian's report;
(6) involvement of your legal representative;
(7) involvement of the court;
(8) closure of the case.

Each section had its own introductory statement that described the theme of a set of questions. Young people were given the opportunity to decide if they wanted to hear the set of questions and/or answer the questions based upon the introductory statement.

### INTERVIEW BOARD GAME

The authority of an adult interviewer can make it difficult for children to opt out of answering questions or an interview altogether. Mahon *et al.* (1996) suggest that:

> The 'problem' of adult authority in relation to children may be more acute when the child and researcher are together on a one-to-one basis. The adoption of more varied and imaginative research methods may make it possible to overcome these problems to some extent; for example, the use of ... imaginative research methods such as video and drawing.                    (p. 149)

A board game was adopted to help children feel sufficiently supported to tell the researcher what they did not wish to talk about. To further support children to opt out of answering questions, kangaroo hops around questions were incorporated into the game.

The decision to use the board game with the younger children was based on the assertion that perception, memory and reasoning are different for children up to 12 years than for adolescents (Weber *et al.*, 1994).

The board game (see Fig. 2) was designed to be used with 8- to 11-year-

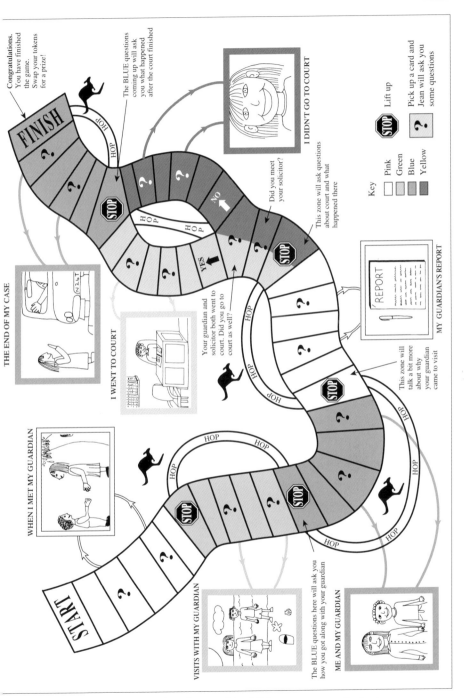

**Fig. 2** *Board game developed to enable children to express their views.*

olds and incorporated all of the questions from the interview schedule, allowing for a comparison of question responses regardless of interview format. In addition it was used by one 12-year-old with mild learning difficulties and one 13-year-old boy after he had briefly seen his younger sibling playing the game.

The board game allowed the interviewer and children to interact in a situation that was familiar to children.

> *Very young children do not, for instance, generally sit and have face-to-face conversations with adults, especially a strange adult. Most conversations occur alongside other activities and usually relate to those activities.* (Beresford, 1997, p. 28)

It was assumed that children would be familiar with playing board games and would be aware of their role of moving objects around the board and answering questions along the way. The adult interviewer could ask questions in a non-threatening manner in keeping with the rules of the game.

The board game format provided a way of visually mapping out a child's involvement with their guardian into sections. A trail was devised that followed the progression of proceedings from the child's first meeting with their guardian, through the court hearing and to the guardian's good-bye visit. The board game was designed in this way in response to an assertion by Beresford (1997) that the 'recall of complex events significantly improves if the event is broken down into a number of simpler units' (p. 25).

Tammivaara and Enright (1986) found that 'Young children generally find doing something with something and talking about that something to be easier, more comfortable, and more interesting than only talking about something that isn't physically present' (p. 232). As such it was hoped that the board game would increase the motivation and maintain the interest of children to participate in the research.

## WORD AND PHRASE CARD GAME

A card game was incorporated into the study because it is an activity that is familiar to children. It provided a natural and non-threatening situation in which the adult interviewer could interact with children.

The word and phrase card game consisted of two parts. Part A assessed what characteristics children perceived an 'ideal' guardian should possess. Part B assessed what children perceived as the characteristics of their own guardian.

Sixteen cards were presented to children in random order:

- Explains things to you
- Doesn't tell you important things
- Is interested in you
- Is not interested in you
- Listens to what you say
- Never listens to what you say
- Gives you time when you want it
- Too busy to see you

- Easy to talk to
- Difficult to talk to
- Gets things done
- Forgets promises
- Helpful
- Useless
- Kind
- Annoying.

Pictures of the child's guardian (drawn by the child), an 'ideal' guardian and a rubbish bin were used with 8- to 11-year-olds. The pictures provided a visual aid to assist children's understanding of what was required of them.

Backett and Alexander (1991) used pictures in a matching game in an examination of children's concepts of healthy foods and activities. Children were asked to post pictures of healthy and unhealthy foods and activities in 'healthy' or 'unhealthy' boxes. The children were then asked to rank seven pictures of activities from the most healthy to the most unhealthy. Due to the abstract nature of the words and phrases in this study it was not possible to use pictures on the cards as Backett and Alexander (1991) did.

For Part A of the card game, 8- to 11-year-olds were introduced to the picture of an 'ideal' guardian and asked to go through the cards and select appropriate words and phrases. Words and phrases that children indicated as inappropriate behaviour for an 'ideal' guardian were placed near the picture of the bin. The children were then asked for their top two choices and whether any words had been missed out.

In Part B, children were asked to point to the words and phrases that described their own guardian. They were then asked whether any words had been missed out.

Parts A and B were presented to children in random order.

## DRAWING AND WRITING EXERCISE

The drawing and writing exercise consisted of a sheet of paper headed 'This paper is for you to write or draw anything you want on'. The purpose of the exercise was to give children the opportunity to express memories, feelings and views of their guardian either overlooked or forgotten during the interview. It also provided a means to express their experience of the interviewers' visit.

The 'write and draw' technique is becoming increasingly popular in research with younger children (e.g. Backett and Alexander, 1991; Levin, 1994; Hill *et al.*, 1996). This technique enables younger children to express their views despite their limited verbal and/or written skills. It also accommodates older children who may feel more adept at providing a written account of their experiences or views.

The 'write and draw' technique was used successfully with children aged 9 and 10 years in a study exploring children's perceptions of cancer (Oakley *et al.*, 1995). The children provided detailed information about their perceptions and beliefs regarding health in general and cancer in particular, illustrating the value of the 'write and draw' technique as a research tool.

## QUESTIONNAIRE FOR GUARDIANS AD LITEM

The guardian questionnaire consisted of 22 questions relating to topics covered in the children's interview. The purpose of the guardians' questionnaire was to elicit a guardian's perspective on their work with a child. Having feedback from guardians would allow us to put the responses of children into context and explain atypical work practices (for example, why a child did not meet her/his solicitor). The guardian questionnaires were not intended to confirm or contradict a child's responses since guardians and children have different perspectives on court proceedings.

## PROCEDURE

The children were aware that the researcher worked for The Children's Society so the researcher was not associated with guardians. It was hoped that by appointing an independent researcher, children would feel able to give an unmodified account of their experience of guardians. We question whether children interviewed by Masson and Winn Oakley (1999) would feel able to discuss freely their views on the guardian service after seeing the interviewer at meetings that they had with their guardian and solicitor.

Research by Koocher and Keith-Spiegel (1994) suggest that children are more sensitive than adults to the personality and appearance of an interviewer. Children may shape their responses according to their expectations of an interviewer (Hill *et al.*, 1996). Therefore, to minimise any potential interviewer bias and to provide consistency, one person (the researcher) conducted all of the interviews.

We intended to interview children within a month of the final hearing, although this was not always possible. The minimum delay between final hearing and interview was 30 days with a maximum of 126 days (approximately 4 months and 6 days). The average delay between final hearing and interview was 74 days (approximately 2 months and 14 days).

Children were given the option of choosing where the interview took place, apart from two young people whom were living in secure accommodation. Interviews were arranged after school and during school holidays.

## *PRE-INTERVIEW*

Before the interview the interviewer introduced herself and asked the children what they knew about the research. They were then told that the researcher was there to find out what they thought about their guardian for a book she was going to write. The children were told that the interviewer wanted to talk to them for about an hour, if they agreed, but they could stop the interview at any time by saying 'I would like to finish this now', or something to that effect. All of the children completed the interview in between 30 minutes and an hour.

Reiterating the introductory letter and leaflet, the children were told that they could bring an adult into the interview at any time during the interview if they wished. Twenty-one children chose to be interviewed without an adult present. It is quite possible that the interview responses of the remaining seven children were influenced by the presence of an adult involved in care proceedings the children were discussing. This needs to be taken into account when analysing their responses.

The children were asked if they were willing to be tape-recorded, on the understanding that the interviewer and possibly her supervisor would hear the tape. Only one young person declined to be taped; on this occasion more detailed notes were taken verbatim.

The children were told that they could change or take out things from the interview record that they did not like or did not want anyone to read. The children were informed that their name and other identifying information would not appear on the interview paperwork or in the book to ensure their anonymity. They were asked to provide a new name to be used instead, which they thoughtfully and enthusiastically did.

The children were informed that the only exception to the guarantee of confidentiality would be if they revealed information suggesting that they or a third party was suffering some form of abuse. This situation did not arise.

Before the interview began the children were given the opportunity to ask the researcher questions. If they were happy to do the interview they were then given a consent form to be signed jointly with an adult.

## CONDUCT OF THE INTERVIEW

At the start of the interview, the interviewer asked each child for her/his guardian's name and what the guardian looked like. To assist 8- to 11-year-olds to focus upon their guardian they were also asked to draw a picture of their guardian.

The interview schedule (or board game for 8- to 11-year-olds) and word and phrase card game were presented in random order. Thirteen children were given the card game first. After the card game and interview schedule the drawing/writing exercise was handed out with a pre-paid envelope for its voluntary return. The children were told that if they wanted they could write or draw what they remembered about their guardian or what they thought of the interview.

## CLOSURE OF THE INTERVIEW

At the end of the interview the children were asked how they felt and whether they wanted further help or support on issues that had arisen during the interview. They were then given a letter to thank them for their participation and to inform them of how they could get in contact with the interviewer. They were also asked to choose from a selection of £5 gift vouchers, to compensate them for their time and effort.

Guardians were sent a questionnaire within a few days of the child's interview.

# CHAPTER 5

# The views of children

In this chapter we will present findings from the children's interviews and games that reveal their experience of what having a guardian was like. We will examine children's views on what makes an 'ideal' guardian, what the role of a guardian is, and whether children felt that they were listened to and understood. References will be made to guardian questionnaire responses where they set the context for the children's comments.

## THE CHARACTERISTICS OF AN 'IDEAL' GUARDIAN

In the word and phrase card game the children were asked to select words and phrases that characterised an 'ideal' guardian. Twenty-three children indicated that guardians should ideally be kind, helpful, easy to talk to and get things done. They should explain things to children, be interested and listen to what children had to say. An 'ideal' guardian should also give children time when they want it.

Three children provided additional information on what an 'ideal' guardian should be like. According to these children a guardian must be 'interesting', 'try to see you more often – should see you once every two weeks' and 'always give you time'.

We wanted to determine what children consider to be the most important characteristics of a guardian. To do this the children were asked to select the 'top two' characteristics that an 'ideal' guardian should possess. Twenty (71%) children said that the most important attribute of a guardian is her/his ability to listen to children. Twelve (43%) children stated that a guardian most importantly should explain things to children. Only a handful of children considered the most important characteristic of a guardian to be: helpful; kind; easy to talk to; interested in children; get things done; or give children time when they want it. Neither age nor gender appeared to influence what children valued most about having a guardian (see Appendix 3).

The twenty-eight children who were interviewed had an expectation of how an 'ideal' guardian should act. The children indicated that most importantly guardians should listen to children and explain things to them. For the remainder of this chapter and also Chapter 6 we will examine how the children's experience of their own guardians compared with their expectations.

## CHILDREN'S UNDERSTANDING OF THE GUARDIAN SERVICE

Fourteen children had a comprehensive understanding of the guardian's role. Both younger and older children were among this group. They knew that the guardian's job was to find out what a child wanted and then speak up for them in court.

*Looking after children and asking them for their opinion ... where do you think you should stay and stuff like that ... In court they would fight for me and they would fight for where I should stay and stuff.*
(Max, 8 years)

*Speak up for them in court. Like say what they want them to say in court. Yeah, she's like a messenger.*
(Chantelle, 15 years)

*Talk to us about what we want to happen and then she was going to go to court and tell my ... solicitor what we wanted and then the solicitor was going to go to court and tell the court what we wanted and then that would help what we wanted to happen.*
(Courtney, 11 years)

*Listens to you and stuff.* [Guardian] *goes to court and speaks on your behalf.*
(Jemma, 11 years)

The remaining 14 children had a limited understanding of the guardian service. Four children thought that their guardian's job was to talk to them.

[Guardian] *helped children that had problems ... by talking to them ... She said she would come, make appointments with us and things and come and see us and take us out and talk to us and things like that.*
(Sarah, 12 years)

Johnny (9 years) and Victoria (8 years) took this further by stating that their guardian talked to them and other people involved with them.

Neither of them could say what their guardian would talk about or why she had gone to see them.

Four children thought that the guardian's role was to help or protect children but couldn't state how guardians did this. Josh (8 years) thought that a 'guardian protects you and lets you know things. They help you know what's going on.' Tim (8 years) said that his guardian looks after children, 'by taking them to nice places like to the park or to the fair.'

The children were asked who had explained the role of the guardian to them. Only the guardian explained the role to most children – they could not remember anyone else describing to them what a guardian was for. Five children remembered that their social worker told them what a guardian did.

*My social worker, she said someone will be coming to meet you. She said they protect you and tell you what's going on.* (Josh, 8 years)

Two siblings recalled that the guardian's 'friend', a solicitor, came and told them what a guardian and solicitor did.

[Solicitor] *said that they help you like ... help you with all the incidents what have happened in your life, what you can remember and all that.* (Matthew, 13 years)

The foster carer or mother of Alice, Joanne and Kirsty explained to them what guardians do.

Most children had a good understanding of a guardian's role. The children knew about various aspects of the guardian's remit, with half having a comprehensive understanding of what guardians do.

## WHOM THE GUARDIAN WORKS FOR

Seven children thought that their guardian worked for social services or their social worker who they knew by first name. These children may have associated their guardian with social services after learning of their first meeting with their guardian through their social worker. However, none of these children had reported in the interview that their social worker had explained the role of a guardian to them.

Some children reported that guardian's work for children or 'people who are in care'. This indicates that children recognise the autonomy of guardians and their role as a representative of children.

A few children associated guardians with working for the court. Victoria (8 years) and Ryan (14 years) stated that their guardian worked for the Guardian Project. Courtney (11 years) said 'A company', Sarah (12 years) thought her solicitor, and Robert (9 years) said that his guardian worked for NCH (Robert had had involvement with a project run by NCH Action for Children).

Eight children were unsure as to whom the guardian worked for. When asked for whom she thought her guardian worked, Chantelle, 15 years, stated:

> I don't know. I don't think she works for anybody does she?

It appears that most guardians did not manage to convey to children that they were associated with either The Children's Society, the court or that they were self-employed. While in itself this might not be important, it is of greater significance that the children did not understand the concept of independence from social services department and family.

### THE USE OF INFORMATION LEAFLETS WITH CHILDREN TO EXPLAIN THE GALRO SERVICE

There are a number of leaflets specifically for children available to guardians at the Humberside GALRO Panel, including those produced by the Humberside Panel and by other panels such as the Inner and North London Panel. The leaflets cover to various degrees the role of the guardian *ad litem*, the children's solicitor and the court. In order to aid their memory in the interview, children were shown all the leaflets known to be used by guardians at the Humberside Panel; they were then asked if they remembered being given a leaflet by their guardian.

Ten children could recall receiving a leaflet on the guardian service. Alice (11 years) remembered that the leaflet

> was yellow and it had a bit at the bottom and it said name and she put 'Alice' ... and it had on it something, a picture or something, in it it had all these sentences about what she was doing.

> I've got it upstairs. It's yellow and it's got like says her name on the front and tells you her telephone number ... it says about guardians and all that and it says her telephone number.      (Jennifer, 10 years)

The guardians of five of these children reported that they had used the leaflet to explain the role of the guardian, which may account for why the children remembered the leaflet so well. One guardian stated that the leaflets are a 'Key tool in explaining the GAL role ... referred back to it periodically throughout work.'

Joanne (11 years) reported that '[Guardian] didn't give one but she gave Mum one.' Joanne couldn't remember having a look at the leaflet. Her guardian reported that with the help of Joanne's mother they went through the leaflet with Joanne in order to explain the role of the guardian. It is possible that at the end of this discussion Joanne's mother took possession of the leaflet.

Seventeen children could not remember their guardian giving them a leaflet. The guardians of only eight of these children could also not recall giving out a leaflet. One guardian explained that two siblings aged 11 and 15 were not given a leaflet because 'I didn't have one to give'. The guardian of an 8-year-old explained that 'One [leaflet] available is not helpful to child's age'. The guardian of one young person in secure accommodation reported that she had very short notice before the first visit so she 'may have forgotten' to give the young person a leaflet.

Of the 17 children who could not remember being given a leaflet, nine had received a leaflet according to their guardian. One guardian reported that the leaflet was sent with the initial appointment letter to two siblings. It is possible that these young people did not receive the letter. It is usual for the leaflets to be given out by guardians at the initial visit with children. For the children interviewed there was a lapse of between 2 and 16 months from the guardian's initial visit to the interview. It is quite understandable that some children would forget receiving a leaflet a number of months previously. Guardians could also have mistakenly remembered giving children a leaflet when they had not done so.

We were interested to see if children who were given a leaflet had a better understanding of the guardian service than those who had not received a leaflet. The extent to which we could answer this question decisively was limited due to the small number of children in each group. However, our examination does provide some indication that receiving a leaflet does not necessarily lead to a greater understanding of the guardian service, on two levels, that of what the guardian's role is and how guardians inform the court of children's wishes and feelings. This can be seen in Table 5 below.

Whether or not children are given a leaflet, they seem to be relatively well informed about the guardian *ad litem* service.

## THE GUARDIAN'S ROLE

### TALKING TO SIGNIFICANT PEOPLE IN CHILDREN'S LIVES
The guardian has a duty under rule 11(9)(a) of the Children Act 1989

*Table 5* Level of understanding of the guardian service for children given and not given a leaflet

| Level of understanding | Children given leaflet ($N = 10$) | Children *not* given leaflet ($N = 8$) |
|---|---|---|
| **Understanding of guardian's role** | | |
| No understanding | 0 | 1 (12.5%) |
| Basic understanding (i.e. GALs talk to children) | 3 (30%) | 2 (25%) |
| Comprehensive understanding (i.e. GALs listen to what children want and tell the court) | 7 (70%) | 5 (62.5%) |
| **Understanding of how guardians inform the court** | | |
| No understanding | 0 | 2 (25%) |
| Basic understanding (i.e. GALs talk to the court) | 4 (40%) | 1 (12.5%) |
| Comprehensive understanding (i.e. GALs write a report to the court or tell the solicitor who informs the court) | 5 (50%) | 4 (50%) |
| Did not answer question | 1 (10%) | 1 (12.5%) |

Guidance and Regulations (1991) to 'contact or seek to interview such persons as he thinks appropriate or as the Court directs' in order to 'develop a comprehensive understanding of the child's needs – physical, psychological, educational, health and development' (Department of Health/Welsh Office, 1995). The guardian must see the child's parents, or those with parental responsibility, and the social worker. Key family members, significant friends, teachers, doctors and other professionals may be seen in order to build up a picture of the child's life and needs. This duty of the guardian is explained to children in various information leaflets for them on the guardian service, such as leaflets produced by the Humberside GALRO Panel and the Inner and North London GALRO Panel.

The children were asked if their guardian had spoken to anyone that they knew about them. Twenty-five children stated that they were aware that their guardian had spoken to others. Most of these children were unsure as to whom their guardian spoke to. They often cited their parents, foster carer, social worker, the judge or court, and solicitors as people their guardian may have spoken to.

> *Probably did but I don't know who, maybe* [social worker], *I know the court, you know the judge and the jury and all that ... She may have spoken to my parents but I don't know.* (Chloe, 14 years)

> *I think she spoke to* [social worker] *... I think she spoke to my grandma and grandad but I don't know ... She told me if she'd be seeing my mum and my grandma in a meeting and my grandad sometimes when he wasn't at work.* (Sarah, 12 years)

Guardians were asked to provide a list of people they actually spoke to in the course of proceedings. The lists included a number of professionals and family members not mentioned by children, such as aunts, uncles, children's home staff, psychologists and psychiatrists. Notably guardians reported speaking to the teachers of 14 children whereas none of these children reported being aware of this. Of these 14 children, nine were aged 11 years or over.

Eight-year-old Josh, who provided well-informed answers throughout the interview, was not aware that his guardian spoke to anyone about him. His guardian reported that she had spoken to Josh's parents, two sets of grandparents, social worker, foster carer and his teacher.

Some children reported that their guardian told them that they had already seen people they knew.

> *She saw them before she saw me I think.* (Michael, 10 years)

Eight children recalled being told beforehand of visits by their guardian to people close to them.

> [Guardian] *just says like I'm going to talk to* [solicitor] *or* [social worker] *or something. She told me who she was going to talk to and she just says is that alright with you.* (Chantelle, 15 years)

> [Guardian] *said, 'Oh I'm going to see whoever.'* (Katie, 14 years)

Chantelle and Katie appear to be well briefed on whom their guardian was going to talk to about them. However, some children could not recall being informed beforehand of visits by their guardian and were not aware of all the people seen by guardians, particularly teachers. It is possible that some children could have forgotten they were told of visits; however, given that at least one child seemed in other respects well informed, it is possible that some guardians may not have informed them.

## VISITS BY THE GUARDIAN WITH CHILDREN

The number of visits to children undertaken by a guardian is determined by the age and understanding of the child, and the complexity and length of proceedings. It is expected that a guardian will see a child at least once (e.g. a baby) but not so often as to develop the closer relationship expected of a social worker. It would be unusual for any guardian to see a child a number of times that reached double figures.

Children were asked a number of questions surrounding their guardians' visits including: how many visits their guardian made to see them; when the guardian visited them; if they were forewarned of the visits; where the visits took place; what happened during the visits; the reason for the visits; and the circumstances surrounding their guardians' last 'good-bye' visit.

### NUMBER OF VISITS

The children remembered their guardian visiting them from two to 22 times.

> About 22 times, maybe more. Probably more than that. It seemed a
> really lot.                                                    (Caroline, 10 years)

The guardian reported visiting Caroline six times. In the interview I checked if Caroline was thinking of her social worker's visits, but was told that '[social worker] came about once a day ... about 30 times, maybe more'.

> [Guardian] came every ... other Wednesday I think ... [it felt like]
> around about 4000 times.                                     (Louise, 11 years)

### TIMING OF VISITS

The majority ($N = 20$) of children were happy with the timing of the guardians' visits. For Katie (14 years) the times were scheduled appropriately 'Cause [guardian] used to ask us what time we'd be in'.

Three young people were not satisfied with when the guardian chose to visit them. Two of these young people were in a secure unit and were seen during school time or their free time.

> It was school time.                                            (John, 12 years)

*You only get from 6 o'clock until I think it's 8.30 when you go for your supper, so that's 2½ hours of your own time, and [guardian] used to come in my time, so I couldn't get goes on computers or homework finished.*  (Ryan, 14 years)

For Courtney, who was 11 years old, the times her guardian visited were fine:

*Apart from one time when it was a Saturday and I used to go and see my mum on a Saturday at 10 o'clock but I couldn't go and see my mum on that day because [guardian] came ... I got to see my mum anyway ... and I think I got to sleep at my mum's that day.*

## PREPAREDNESS FOR VISITS

Guardians have a specific duty to assess the wishes and feelings of children and will usually see children alone on at least one occasion, particularly with children in this age range.

Most of the children were told when their guardian was coming to visit them. For 11 children a foster carer, parent or grandparent who lived with them informed them of their guardian's intended visit.

*My mum told me that they [guardian] were coming whenever and I had to be in at that time.*  (Matthew, 13 years)

Ryan (14 years), who was living in a secure unit was told by the staff of his guardian's visits:

*The first time I got told and the second time and I think it was the last time, but I think they told me all the time.*

Eight children were informed by the guardian when they would next be visiting them through letters or by booking the next visit when about to leave.

*[Guardian] would write a letter to me to tell me when she was coming around. She'd say, 'Dear Chantelle, I've made arrangements for to see you on this day. If you need to change it just ring me on this number. See you soon.'*  (Chantelle, 15 years)

*[Guardian] just writes like a love letter when she's coming ... It was like a postcard.*  (Louise, 11 years)

*Guardian used to book it before she left the last time.*
(Jamie Lee, 15 years)

For five children the guardian's visits were a surprise, as they could not remember anyone informing them of the intended visits. Two of these children were living in a secure unit or a residential unit. The short notice of secure accommodation applications would account for this at initial interviews, but not subsequent ones.

> It surprised me ... nobody told me. Apart from the day she was coming. She just arrived and then they went 'this is your guardian.'
> (Alan, 11 years)

Alan reported that every time his guardian came it was like this.

> I was surprised.
> (John, 12 years)

John's experience of unexpected visits by the guardian was mirrored in his experience of the researcher's visit. When the researcher went to visit John he was surprised to see her and asked who she was and why she had come. It appears that letters to John confirming the interview were not forwarded to him.

Robert and Kirsty, both 9 years old and living with their mother, were surprised each time their guardian came to visit them. Max, aged 8 years and living with his grandparents, was similarly surprised. This would suggest that guardians cannot rely on adult carers to inform children of planned visits and reinforces the need to communicate directly, as with Chantelle, Louise and Jamie Lee (above).

## PLACE AND CONTENT OF VISITS

The guardians' visits were usually held where the child was currently living. The children also enjoyed visits to McDonalds and other restaurants with their guardian. The children recalled that the visits involved a lot of talking on both parts and answering the questions of their guardian.

> [Guardian] asked us questions and asked us if we wanted to ask her questions. She'd give us leaflets and things and I don't know what else. We went to McDonalds as well.
> (Sarah, 12 years)

> [Guardian] asked me how old I was, if I was alright, if I was OK, if I was happy living with my grandma and grandad, if I was happy, if I was just happy ... she was just there to talk about if I was happy.
> (Lisa, 8 years)

> [Guardian] just asked us what we'd like to happen in the future.
> (Courtney, 11 years)

Five children remembered their guardian playing games with them to find out what they wanted and what people were important to them.

*We played this card game ... you had to put out like who you wanted to live with and all that.* (Matthew, 13 years)

*At school* [guardian] *played a little game about what I was thinking about everything that was going on. She had faces: troubled ones, happy ones, worried ones and sad ones.* (Max, 8 years)

[Guardian] *got a woman and it opened up and other women came out.* (Alice, 11 years)

Max's guardian reported using Russian dolls with him as had Alice's guardian. Russian dolls are used by guardians to determine children's views of the strength of relationships from different perspectives between themselves, their parents, foster carers, and members of their extended family or other significant people in their lives. They also examine the balance of power in relationships. Expressive faces are used to evaluate what attributes children accord themselves or other people in different situations, for example, how they feel when they visit their mother or father, and how people close to them appear. The use of varied techniques to engage with children enables guardians to explore a child's view of her/his situation and relationship with family members. These games and exercises are particularly useful with younger children, which may account for there being only five children who reported their use in our sample.

### REASON FOR VISITS

Most children thought that the reason their guardian visited them was to find out what they wanted to happen to them, such as who they wanted to live with and be able to see. Some children related this to the court, stating that their guardian would tell the court what they wanted. The children's understanding of the reason for the guardian's visits reflected what they had said about the role of the guardian.

*To talk about what's going to happen at court and what* [guardian] *thinks should happen and what I think should happen.*

(Ryan, 14 years)

[Guardian] *said that my dad had put in for a court order, a residence, well one where I can live with him or something, a residence order or something. And she said that she wanted to listen to what I wanted to happen with the residence.* (Claire, 13 years)

*[Guardian] was trying to get information about us ... How you're getting along with your mum and dad.*                    (Josh, 8 years)

## THE GUARDIAN'S GOOD-BYE VISIT

We wanted to ascertain whether the children were aware in advance that the guardian's involvement would stop after the final hearing. The children were asked when they thought their guardian would stop seeing them.

Sixteen children stated that they thought their guardian would stop seeing them after the court hearing had finished.

*When all this social services stopped and when we didn't need [guardian] and when court all finished and that.*    (Caroline, 10 years)

*Until it was all over ... When we've got the residence order.*
(Lisa, 8 years)

*Once [guardian] had been, when she had been to court they arranged it ... to make us not go to see her anymore.*           (Tim, 8 years)

Some or all of these children may have known that their guardian would stop seeing them after the court hearing because it had already happened. They may not have been forewarned or prepared for the guardian's limited involvement. It was considered too difficult for young children to specify at what point in the proceedings they were told that their guardian would stop seeing them after the final hearing. The young people who were asked stated that they were informed:

*right at the end* [of proceedings].              (Chantelle, 15 years)

*in the middle* [of proceedings].               (Jamie Lee, 15 years)

*inside the court* [last day of court].                 (John, 12 years)

Joanne, who was 11 years old, 'never thought [guardian] would stop seeing me until she told us ... a few weeks ago I think. Yeah, a few weeks ago ... She told me on that day, we never knew till that day, but mum knew before.'

Nine-year-old Johnny reported that he wasn't forewarned that his guardian's involvement would end.

*[Guardian] never said anything, she just stopped seeing me.*

Likewise Alice wasn't forewarned that she would stop seeing her guardian, but she knew that she wasn't going to come back after she had a good-bye visit from her guardian.

Alan (11 years) thought that he would stop seeing his guardian 'when I am in my early 20s'. Robert (9 years) said that 'Two years later [after the final hearing]' his guardian would stop seeing him. The guardians of these two boys reported making a good-bye visit on the day of the final hearing at court and home, respectively.

Six younger children were not sure when they thought their guardian would stop seeing them despite all but one stating at the end of the interview that they had a good-bye visit.

### No good-bye visits

Four children could not remember their guardian saying a final farewell to them. They all expected their guardian to visit them again, if only to say good-bye. Courtney and Jamie Lee's guardian reported that she had said good-bye to the girls days before the final hearing and wished them all the best. However the girls expected another visit from their guardian to say a formal farewell.

> [Guardian] *came the day before they went to court and she said I'll come and see you one day after the court but she didn't come ... It might be because she's busy or it might be because she lives so far away.*                                         (Courtney, 11 years)

> [Guardian] *was actually supposed to come back after the court hearing to say a proper good-bye but she never.*          (Jamie Lee, 15 years)

Paul's guardian stated that she had not made a good-bye visit as she 'did not have an opportunity or the time to say good-bye after the final hearing' because she went on leave soon after the hearing. Four months after the hearing Paul was still waiting for a visit from his guardian and told me 'she might be coming soon.'

The response of these children illustrates how important it is for guardians to be clear about the ending of their involvement with a particular child, ensuring that the child understands this.

### Venue of good-bye visit

The majority of children (N = 23) remembered vividly their guardian's good-bye visit. Most visits occurred in the child's home. The four children who attended the final hearing or spoke to the judge after the hearing said good-bye to their guardian at court. The guardians of five young people chose to mark the occasion by making a special trip to a restaurant.

> [Guardian] *took us out to dinner, me and* [sibling] *... we went for a meal and then she bought us two presents ... Then she gave us a big hug in the middle of the street.*    (Chantelle, 15 years)

> Yeah [guardian] *took me to McDonalds. I think she came with my solicitor as well.*    (Claire, 13 years)

### TIMING OF GOOD-BYE VISIT

Most good-bye visits took place either on the day of the final hearing or a few days afterwards. Alice's guardian said good-bye with her solicitor four weeks after the final hearing.

> [Guardian] *came around one day the last time with* [...] *the solicitor and we talked a bit and then she went and she said good-bye.*
> (Alice, 11 years)

Alice's guardian did not explain why there was a delay in visiting Alice. However, her guardian did ensure that Alice's social worker would tell her the outcome of the final hearing immediately.

One guardian made a good-bye visit 3 months after the final hearing, as this was appropriate to the family's current circumstances. A letter was written to the young person saying farewell in the meantime.

## BEING LISTENED TO AND HEARD/UNDERSTOOD

### LISTENED TO

At the beginning of this chapter we reported that children considered that one of the most important characteristics of an 'ideal' guardian was their ability to listen to children. We wanted to examine whether the children felt that their guardian listened to them and their reasons for feeling this.

Twenty-five children thought that their guardian did listen to them.

Seven children knew that their guardian was listening because their guardian repeated what they had said, talked about it or asked questions about what they had said.

> *Because she kept answering me back.*    (Josh, 8 years)

Alan, who was 11 years old, tested his guardian to see if she was listening to him, 'I asked [guardian] what I'd said and she told me exactly what I'd said.'

For six children they knew their guardians were listening because the guardians wrote down what they had said to them.

*Because she was, she was writing it all down on a piece of paper.*

(Kirsty, 9 years)

*Well she sort of like wrote down the stuff I was saying.*

(Michael, 10 years)

Six children surmised that their guardians were listening to them because they were looking at them.

*Because she kept looking at me and wasn't ignoring me.*

(Johnny, 9 years)

*Because she had her ears open. I could tell she was listening when she was looking at me.* (Paul, 11 years)

For four young people they knew their guardians were listening because the guardians answered their questions either immediately or at their next meeting.

*Because if I asked* [guardian] *a question she'd answer it the way I wanted her to answer it, and she'd answer it, she wouldn't ignore it. And if I said something she'd say 'yeah' or 'right' like you. Or sometimes she'd write it down.* (Caroline, 10 years)

*Because when she came back she always came back and said ... the answers.* (Alice, 11 years)

Courtney, who was 11 years old, knew that her guardian was listening to her because 'she went back and told my solicitor and the solicitor went to tell the court what we wanted and we got to come home'. Robert, who was 9 years old, wasn't sure why he thought that his guardian was listening to him.

The majority of children who were interviewed valued being listened to by their guardian and knew that they weren't being ignored. Chloe, who was 14 years old, epitomised the enthusiasm and surprise of the children of being listened to when she stated, 'well [guardian] was listening and she used to focus on what you were saying so you really could think this is good this listening'.

Three children did not feel that they were sufficiently listened to by their guardians. They each had different guardians. Claire, who was 13 and living in a residential unit, thought that her guardian listened to her *about half the time ... when I was saying things to* [guardian] *she was like talking to my* [sibling] *... and she'd just ignore me and talk to my* [sibling] *and things and change the subject.*

John, who was 12 and living in a secure unit, said that his guardian

*wasn't really paying attention to what I was saying. She was just like listening to my social worker ... in court. When I was at court she wasn't really listening to me. When I met her* [at secure unit] *she listened but not much.*

Eight-year-old Max stated that his guardian listened to sport on the radio on one visit instead of listening to him.

### HEARD/UNDERSTOOD

Twenty-two children thought that their guardian had understood what they wanted. All but one girl, age 8, who couldn't remember exactly what she had told her guardian, reported that their guardians understood where they wanted or didn't want to live and/or whom they wanted or didn't want to see.

*That I wanted to live with my mum and dad and it hurts and she understood, that's it.*

*Well I told* [guardian] *that I just wanted to come back home to my mum. And that's what she went and told the court and the court let us come home.*

When Paul (11 years) was asked if his guardian understood what he wanted he initially stated, 'I don't know because I am not in her brain', but upon deliberation he concluded that his guardian did understand because 'I told her that I wanted to live here [in foster home], at least I got to live here.'

Surprisingly 8-year-old Max, who had said that his guardian had not listened to him, thought that his guardian did understand what he wanted. I checked this out with him and twice he confirmed his belief that his guardian understood that 'I wanted to live here [at grandparents house] sometimes and at my mum's some other times'. It may be that she had listened to Max sufficiently for him to believe that his wishes were understood.

Four children thought that their guardian had not sufficiently understood what they wanted to happen to them and why. Not surprisingly, two of these young people, Claire and John, had reported that their guardian had not listened to them either.

John thought that no one understood what he really wanted:

*I have like wishes and feelings and I write it down there* [in a booklet from the social worker]. *No one looks at it. It's only the judges that look at it and the magistrates.*

John told his guardian what he wanted

*but I don't think she was really bothered. All she was just bothered about was getting me a* [secure accommodation] *order.*

Claire stated:

*I said that I didn't want to live with my dad. She understood that but then I told her not to tell him that I said that and she went and told him. I wanted contact with* [my dad] *but not so much, not loads of contact. She understood that bit. Well she didn't understand that I didn't want to stay with my dad, live with my dad and she just ... was like saying that 'why don't you want to live with your dad?' and everything. I just kept saying 'I don't want to' and she kept asking me.*

It is concerning that Claire was not aware that her guardian could not keep her wishes confidential.

Like Claire, Alice thought that her guardian did not understand why she did not want to live with one of her parents. Alice stated:

*It's just sometimes I don't think she understood ... I know* [guardian] *wanted me to go to stay with mum. She didn't understand why I didn't want to go and stay with mummy.*

We were interested to see to what extent children felt not listened to nor understood if the court did not follow their wishes and feelings. There were 11 children who did not get what they had wished for at the end of the proceedings. Where the children were subject to secure accommodation proceedings reactions are understandable. What this research does illustrate is that standards of practice can be variable in this area, and how important it is for guardians to have the skills to both assess wishes and feelings and to explain why recommendations may be different, in terms of welfare and based on the guardian's own assessment. Nine of these children reported that they felt listened to and understood by their guardian. John and Claire felt that their guardians had listened to them only some of the time and did not understand their wishes and feelings. It appears that most children feel listened to and understood despite not having their wishes followed.

AGREEMENT AND DISAGREEMENT BETWEEN CHILDREN'S WISHES AND GUARDIAN'S RECOMMENDATIONS TO THE COURT

Ten children believed that their guardian agreed that what they wanted should happen. These children varied in age and all recognised that their guardian agreed with what they wanted because it was in their best interest. Some showed insight into the reasons why this was best for them.

> *She thought that it was alright and she thought that I was safe and better off here.*
> (Lisa, 8 years)

> *She thought it was right. What we wanted was best really.*
> (Katie, 14 years)

Seven children thought that their guardian disagreed that what they wanted should happen. Three of these children remembered their guardian explaining to them why they could not recommend to the court what they wanted.

> [Jennifer's guardian] *just said well you can't go back home or you might get hurt.*
> (Jennifer, 10 years)

> [Guardian] *knew that I wanted to be out* [of secure unit] *for Christmas but she said the way I was responding to her questions she thought I should have another three-month order.*
> (Ryan, 14 years)

Two sisters remembered their guardian telling them that they would probably not be able to go home as they wished.

> *I told* [guardian] *that I wanted to go home but it wasn't really necessary that I could go home. Like I knew that I was going to have a court case and I knew that we wouldn't be able to go home.*
> (Jemma, 11 years)

> *I am sure she had a feeling that it wouldn't happen but she still, well she didn't exactly gave me hope making me think that well yes it's going to happen but she gave me the truth.*
> (Chloe, 14 years)

Eleven-year-old Alice believed that her guardian wanted her to live with her mum, whereas she wanted to live with her foster carer. However, her guardian stated that she agreed with Alice that she should live with her foster carer.

Five children could not remember their guardian telling them whether they agreed or disagreed with their wishes.

> *She was very secretive.*
> (Claire, 13 years)

*She didn't say.* (Victoria, 8 years)

*I don't know what she actually thought. She didn't really say.*
(Jamie Lee, 15 years)

It may be that some guardians are particularly cautious about expressing their own views during the course of their assessment, or indeed they may not have formulated their views. These responses illustrate that guardians should be mindful of the need to check with children that they know the guardian will be reflecting their wishes and feelings but that the guardian also has a duty to assess best interests in line with the paramountcy principle. Keeping the child suitably informed would seem to be consistent with that principle.

Interestingly in their own questionnaires the guardians of Claire, Victoria, Jamie Lee and Alice stated that they agreed that what the children wanted was in their best interests and was recommended by them to the court.

For David and Paul, their guardians were non-committal about their view on them wanting to live with their parents and mother, respectively.

*She said we'd have to wait and see.* (David, 12 years)

*She said she had a lot to think about.* (Paul, 11 years)

David and Paul's guardians reported that they did not support their view that they should live back at home. It may have been difficult for their guardians to explain this clearly to them, especially since both boys had learning difficulties. This highlights the need for guardians to find other methods of communication to reinforce information for children with learning difficulties.

Overall it appears that guardians are able to communicate clearly to children their reasons why they could or could not support children's wishes.

## THE CHARACTERISTICS OF THE CHILDREN'S OWN GUARDIANS

A benefit of the word and phrase card game was that it reinforced what children had said in the interview. This adds validity to the findings of the interview because the children repeated views expressed in the interview. For example when the interviews were positive the children provided these extra words to describe their guardian in the card game:

*Tried to really help me. She really cared about what she was doing.*

*Happy, funny, always got nice things to say.*

*Really, really, really kind.*

*Caring.*

Fourteen (52%) children attributed all of the positive words and phrases in the card game to their guardian, that is, the characteristics of an 'ideal' guardian. They saw their guardian as being interested in them, a good listener who explained things to them, gave them time and was easy to talk to. They attributed no negative characteristics to their guardian, which was reiterated in their interviews.

Five children used the word and phrase card game to reiterate criticisms about their guardian's conduct that were revealed in the interview.

Jamie Lee reported that her guardian forgot a promise made to her. She repeated what she had said during the interview, that her guardian 'said she was going to come back to say good-bye but didn't'.

Claire (13 years) reported that her guardian forgot promises, was 'difficult to talk to' and was 'sometimes annoying' and didn't tell her important things. Claire added that her guardian 'sometimes told me things and they weren't true'. Claire may have been referring to the letter sent by her guardian after the final hearing, which was discussed in the interview.

Ryan (14 years) characterised his guardian as being 'difficult to talk to', 'annoying' and 'useless' (possibly because he got a secure order when he did not want one). He reported that his guardian did not tell him important things, or get things done. He said that his guardian did not give him time when he had wanted it, reflecting his comment in the interview that his guardian visited him during his free time in the secure unit.

Twelve-year-old John reiterated a number of complaints using the card game that came up in the interview. He stated that his guardian was too busy to see him, did not give him time when he wanted it and never listened to what he said. When his guardian 'wasn't paying attention' he found it difficult to talk to his guardian, but when she was paying attention it was easy. According to John his guardian did not 'get things done' (he wanted to go to a children's home but was placed in a secure unit), did not explain things to him, nor was she interested in him. John did not think that his guardian was 'kind'.

Eight-year-old Max reported that his guardian was too busy to see him and did not give him time when he wanted it. His guardian was 'annoying', not interested in him, did not get things done and did not explain things to him.

These responses, from five out of 28 children, represent a high proportion of the sample. The comments also cover a range of dissatisfactions. There are specific lessons for the quality of practice and this illustrates the value of feedback from children as a means of monitoring and developing good practice; this will be referred to again in Chapter 9.

## CONCLUSION

A surprising finding was that the children had little or no understanding of whom the guardian worked for. Interestingly, while this had significance for the researcher in terms of unexpected outcomes, it actually seemed to have little relevance for the children. Even when children thought the guardian worked for the social services department this did not impede them from feeling listened to or understanding explanations. Nevertheless, the consistency of this finding has implications for guardians' explanations to children in future about their role.

The research showed that only a limited number of guardians seemed to use leaflets, but also that for the few children who had seen the leaflets (and most could identify where the leaflet was in their current home), this did not seem particularly to enhance their understanding.

The children's understanding of what guardians do was good; this was consistent across the age range. Despite this the children had a limited understanding of whom the guardian would actually speak to. They were almost all aware the guardian would speak to highly significant professionals, parents, the social worker, foster carer and sometimes the solicitor and/or the judge. They were not aware of the guardian talking to others, including teachers and current residential care staff.

On the whole the children knew the guardian's role was time-limited, but by no means all understood this.

All the children who were prepared for a visit by their guardian appreciated this, and all appreciated being given choice about the appropriate time for a future visit.

For many of the children, the most significant characteristics of the guardian were her/his ability to listen to children and to explain things to them. The children were very clear that they felt listened to and understood. They were also aware of the guardian's recommendations to the court and the reasons for it.

# 6

# Children's experience of the court process

Having given children's views on guardians, we now examine children's views of the court process in order to understand how guardians may have affected their experiences of this. We will examine children's understanding of their guardian's role in the process, the nature of their interaction with the court and their understanding of the court's decision. References will be made to guardian questionnaire responses where it sets the context for children's comments.

## CONVEYING CHILDREN'S WISHES AND FEELINGS TO THE COURT

### CHILDREN'S UNDERSTANDING OF HOW GUARDIANS INFORM THE COURT

Two children, Alan (11 years old) and Kirsty (9 years old), were unsure as to whether their guardian told the court what they wanted.

Five children declined to answer this series of questions on the guardian's report. The remaining 21 children knew that their guardian conveyed what they wanted to the court and most ($N = 17$) had an understanding of how they did this. Four children did not know how their guardian informed the court of where they wanted to live and/or whom they wanted to see. Two of these children reported that they did not know this because they had not gone to court.

Nine children knew that their guardian conveyed their wishes and feelings to the court by talking to the judge or magistrates. I checked with these young people if the guardian only talks to the court or whether they write things also. They reported that the guardian only talks to the court.

> She'd go up to them and say [Jennifer] *wants to come back but we can't let her.*
> (Jennifer, 10 years)

*I think she'd tell the court the way I said it and put it in a bit more complicated words what I can't say ... Tell them actually in court.*

(Joanne, 11 years)

[Guardian] *stands up and tells them what you want to do.*

(Josh, 8 years)

Four young people reported that their guardian writes to the court to convey their wishes and feelings. They did not mention by name the guardian's report.

*Well, we draw pictures and write and* [guardian] *writes stuff and that and* [guardian] *shows the court stuff.*

(Jemma, 11 years)

[Guardian] *gave them* [the court] *a little slip that said what I want and what I don't want ... * [guardian] *wrote it ... When she took us to McDonalds she didn't bring anything because she said when I go ... home she was going to write it all down.*

(Louise, 11 years)

*She'd told 'em everything what we said to her and she said it like the same way ... she used to write things about what we said and she used to write it down.*

(Matthew, 13 years)

Four young people were adamant that the guardian did not inform the court what they wanted directly as that duty belonged to their solicitor. They thought the guardian passed messages from the children to the court through the solicitor.

*Well* [guardian] *wouldn't tell the court but my solicitor would tell the court ... * [Guardian] *would go to the solicitor and she'd tell the solicitor what we've said and the solicitor would go and tell the court.*

(Courtney, 11 years)

[Guardian would] *write everything down what we'd say then talk to* [solicitor] *and* [solicitor] *would say it.*

(Katie, 14 years)

[Guardian would] *not actually tell them herself because that's what the solicitor is for.*

(Jamie Lee, 15 years)

## THE GUARDIAN'S REPORT

Before asking questions on the guardian's report the 23 children who agreed to answer these questions were told, in an age-appropriate manner, that the guardian wrote a report for the court, which included a section on their wishes and feelings. Twenty children believed that their guardian knew them well enough to write down for the court what they wanted to happen to them and why. Courtney, who was 11 years old, reported that her guardian:

> *knew us a bit but not a lot. But she knew us well enough to do a report.*

This question links back to the children's views on whether their guardian understood what they wanted to happen to them. In the main children who believed that their guardian understood what they wanted were confident that their guardian could write an appropriate report to the court on their wishes. Thirteen-year-old Matthew was the only young person to report that his guardian understood what he wanted but then later stated that he felt that his guardian did not know him well enough to write a report on his wishes and feelings. He believed that sometimes he did not explain to his guardian adequately what he wanted but 'sometimes I know I told her it right'.

Alice, who was 11 years old, believed that her guardian could write an adequate report for the court on what she wanted despite feeling that her guardian did not fully understand her reasons for not wanting to live with her mother.

Claire and John, who had both believed that their guardian did not understand what they wanted, unsurprisingly reported that their guardian would not be able to adequately state their wishes and feelings in a report for the court. They both thought that their guardians did not know them well enough to do a report on them because they had not spent enough time with them.

> *She hardly came and seen me or know much about me really.*
>
> (John, 12 years)

> *She could have spent a little bit more time with me and talked about like what I do ... just a little bit more time.*    (Claire, 13 years)

Claire also reported that she felt restricted in what she could tell her guardian because there were other people in the room with them.

> *When* [guardian] *used to come around my step-dad used to be there and he used to be there and* [guardian] *didn't say can we have it private, he used to be sat in the room.*

The implications of this, and other practice issues, will be discussed in Chapters 8 and 9. However, reference has already been made to an assumption that children will have the opportunity to speak to their guardian on their own.

The children were asked if their guardian had either shown them or talked to them about what was written in the guardian's report. Five children remembered seeing parts of the guardian's report or documents that were going into the report.

Matthew remembered that the report was:

*In a booklet thing, in a like a folder. Yeah and she showed us it, she got it out and showed us it ... I thought it were alright.*

*Well she showed me once and I had a little look at it and she said this is what I'm going to give to the court.* (Lisa, 8 years)

Chantelle provides an example of why guardians must be careful when showing young people their report:

[Guardian] *did get them* [things in the report] *right but I just didn't want to hear them kind of things. But it was right.* (Chantelle, 15 years)

Five children remembered their guardian describing to them what was written in some of the report.

*She didn't show* [the report] *to us but she said bits and that. She said that I'd done a report and it had gone to the Court.* (Katie, 14 years)

*She didn't go through it properly she just said what she'd put down but not all of it.* (Claire, 13 years)

Twelve children did not remember either seeing or hearing about what their guardian had put in their report. However, some of the guardians of these children reported reading parts of the report to them or verbally explaining what they had written to the children.

## CHILDREN'S ATTENDANCE AT COURT

### CHILDREN WHO WANTED TO GO TO COURT AND DID

Fifteen children stated that they wanted to go to court. Nine of them did so by either attending the final hearing ($N = 2$), attending a directions hearing ($N = 2$), visiting an empty courtroom ($N = 3$) or talking to the judge after the hearing ($N = 2$). The majority ($N = 6$) of these young people went to the County Court. Three young people went to a Family Proceedings Court, with two involved in final hearings for secure accommodation applications.

Thirteen-year-old Claire went to a directions hearing but wanted to also go to the final hearing. Her solicitor and guardian 'wouldn't let me go, they just said it was best not to.' Claire wanted to go to the final hearing because 'I just wanted to see what had been said instead of being told by a letter [from her guardian and social worker] that I thought wasn't true.'

Jemma, who was 11 years old, remembered her visit to the County Court: '[Social worker] actually took us and we met [guardian] there and then this other lady came and pretended to be the judge and we went into where you talk, we all had a go and if I went in [social worker, guardian and two siblings] would ask me questions.'

Of the nine children who attended court, six remembered someone telling them what being in court would be like. The guardian of four children described the court set-up.

> [Guardian] *said stuff like what happens, the guardian, all the solicitors.* [Guardian] *and* [solicitor] *talk to the judges and the social workers.*
> (Katie, 14 years)

Michael, who was 10 years old, remembered his foster sister and foster mother telling him what to expect on his visit to court.

> [My sister] *said it was a small room and you go in with your mum and dad and some other people. I can't remember who the people was in the room but she told me that there was people there ... it was like what she said. Well my mum told me practically the same thing.*

Ryan was able to learn about the Family Proceedings Court from visiting his friends in the waiting area of the court.

> *Some of my friends, you know before I come in here* [secure unit] *they knew, when they went to court for an order they'd phone us up and say, 'Oh I'm going to court on a Thursday or somethin' and 'go' and I'd go to the family court and talk to 'em, pretend like I was going into the family court but talk to them instead because the escorts usually take them from here and from other secure units and I would've been waiting there.*

Three young people could not remember being told beforehand what the court would be like. Of concern, two of these young people, Claire and John, were present at court hearings, directions and final hearings, respectively.

Only two young people, both in a secure final hearing, reported hearing what their guardian had to say about them in court. Ryan thought that his guardian explained what he wanted to the court 'right'.

All nine children who went to court were glad that they had gone. Max thought that going to see the empty courtroom was 'No big deal. It was pretty good. I climbed a tree in the car park.'

### CHILDREN WHO WANTED TO GO TO COURT AND DID NOT

There were six children who wanted to go to court but did not, of whom four were involved in proceedings in the Family Court and two at County Court level. Excluding secure accommodation proceedings, where young people must attend hearings, 80% of children who wanted to go to the Family Court were not given the opportunity to attend. This compares to 25% in the County Court.

Of the children who did not see the court, their guardian and/or carer told three children that they couldn't go because they were too young.

*My Nanna told me it was just for big people ...* [Guardian] *said that it wasn't a place for me, she said that no children could go there, only if it's bad.*                                      (Lisa, 8 years)

[Guardian] *said I was too young.*                        (Josh, 8 years)

[Didn't go] *Because I was too young.* [My foster carer] *said I was, because I wasn't twelve.*                          (Alice, 11 years)

Courtney said that she was 'never asked if I wanted to go' (11 years). Joanne and Louise, who were both 11 years old, were not sure why they did not go to court. Their guardians reported that the girls were 'too young' to go to court.

The children who did not attend court had clear reasons why they needed and wanted to attend court.

*Because I just wanted to go and see what they did at court and what happened.*                                      (Courtney, 11 years)

*So to see what they were doing.*                        (Louise, 11 years)

*Because I wanted to tell them what I wanted in my own words.*
                                                          (Josh, 8 years)

With hindsight three children were glad that they had not been able to go to court. Courtney was glad she had not gone to court:

*Because when* [sibling] *went she said that it wasn't very nice, because she got told everything that had been happening for the year and why me and* [younger sibling] *had gone into care and all that.*

Lisa (8 years) was glad that she hadn't gone to court:

*Otherwise I would have just been sat there listening to all they said and nothing to do. And I'm glad I stayed with my friends and played.*

Josh, who was 8 years old, still wished that he had been given the opportunity to go to court 'because I wanted to go'. Eleven-year-olds Alice and Joanne had mixed feelings about not going to court. Joanne said, 'I'm a bit glad that I didn't go and a bit sad.'

Overall the majority of children who wanted to go to court were given the opportunity to do so. However, there were six children who were not given the opportunity to go to court, nor to visit the court as a means of understanding the process.

### CHILDREN WHO DID NOT WANT TO GO TO COURT

Ten children did not want to go to court. Only Matthew and Sarah sought to explain why.

*Because I was too scared.*                    (Matthew, 13 years)

*Because it would put a bit of pressure on me I think and I'd get a bit upset and confused I think.*                    (Sarah, 12 years)

Most of the children who didn't want to go to court could remember being told what court was like. Three siblings were shown around the court but decided that they did not want to be present at the hearings. Matthew's guardian told him that the court was a place 'where like no one can hurt you and all this and it would be safe for me to go'. Paul's mother 'just said the judge sits in the middle and all the people sit at the sides'.

They all reported that they were glad that they hadn't gone to court.

## THE COURT'S DECISION

### HOW CHILDREN LEARNED ABOUT THE COURT'S DECISION

Thirteen children were told by their guardian what the court had decided. For four children their guardian was the only person they could remember who informed them of the court's decision. Their guardian and grandmother told two children. Seven children were told of the outcome by their guardian and social worker, although not necessarily together at the same time. Four children were informed about the court's decision by their social worker only. Four were told by their parent or grandparent only. These sources of information are summarised in Table 6.

John and Ryan were in court and so directly learnt of the magistrate's decision regarding their secure order. John's social worker and solicitor explained the outcome to him as he 'didn't understand what they [the magistrates] were saying'. John reported that his guardian was not there as 'she was sat next to my mum.'

Four children could not remember who told them about the court's decision and one child declined to answer this question.

There are practice implications here for guardians which may be related to issues about good-bye visits and how children perceive the role of the guardian, which we will discuss in Chapters 8 and 9.

**Table 6** *How children learned of the court's decision*

| Decision explained by: | Number of children |
| --- | --- |
| Guardian only | 4 |
| Guardian + social worker | 7 |
| Guardian + grandparent | 2 |
| Social worker only | 4 |
| Parent or grandparent only | 4 |
| Magistrates | 2 |
| Can't remember | 4 |
| Declined to answer | 1 |

## CHILDREN'S UNDERSTANDING OF THE COURT'S DECISION

Most of the children interviewed had an understanding of how the court's decision affected them – that is, where they could live and who they could see. In order to protect the identity of the children interviewed names will not be included with the following interview extracts.

The children had a range of interpretations of what the effect would be on their lives if a care order was made. Three young people, who had the same guardian, were aware that at age 16 they could move out of foster care. Those with a limited understanding of care orders at least knew where the court decided they should live and whom they could see.

*That we have to stay in foster care until we're 16. And that we'd still be seeing our mum like and* [siblings] *but won't be living with mum and dad.*

*We can't go home...we had to keep in care until we're 16 I think.*

*They said that I'd have to live with my grandma and that I'd see my mum once a month.*

The children who were subject to either a residence, discharge of care, contact and/or supervision order had a good understanding of what these orders meant to them in terms of where they could live and whom they could have contact with.

*They decided that I should stay with my Nanna.*

*They decided that I should live with my dad. Mum was an alcoholic and we shouldn't live with her.*

*Stay with my Nanna until my mum is fit to be a mum.*

*They said they'd take us off the register and we could live with our mum and we could see my dad.*

The two young people who were subject to secure accommodation orders knew that this meant a stay in a secure unit for at least 3 months.

*They gave me a 3 month order. I didn't want that, I only wanted a month or something.*

*That they were going to apply for a 3 month order and then I'd go back to court and see if I get another order.*

### CHILDREN'S RESPONSE TO THE COURT'S DECISION

Fourteen children were happy with the court's decision as it complied with what they had wanted throughout the course of the proceedings. One young person had been placed on a care order as she wished because she wanted to live with her siblings in foster care. However, her care order had not been followed and she was living with her parents while her siblings remained in foster care.

Ten children reported that the outcome of their court case was not what they wanted. Eight of these children wanted to go home to live with one or both parents or in a children's home but were placed in a secure unit, residential unit or foster home.

*[Wanted] to have a supervision order ... It means that you can go home but you ... if you need someone to talk to you can see people at the social worker's place.* (This young person was placed in foster care)

*I wanted to go in a children's home instead of secure.*

*I did want to stay at home with my mum.*

(This young person was placed in a residential unit)

One young person was living with one of her parents when she wanted ideally to live with them both together. She stated:

*I always knew that I wouldn't get them back together ever because my mum ... has someone and my dad has someone.*

Three children were not asked this question as it was not appropriate and one child declined to answer it.

## CONCLUSION

Most children knew the guardian informed the court and how the guardian did this. They knew the guardian talked to judges (or 'the court') about their wishes and feelings (some were aware the guardian talked to the solicitor also who informed the court). None spontaneously mentioned the guardian's report but when directly asked, only a few had seen it or had had part of it read to them.

Twenty children believed the guardian knew them well enough to reflect accurately wishes and feelings in the report. There was a clear link here with feeling understood. In the main, those who felt understood were confident the guardian could write a report about their wishes and feelings.

Concerning going to court, of the 25 children who answered this question 15 wanted to go, but only nine did, this nine including those who were shown the court while empty or who spoke to the judge afterwards. Only two children attended the final hearing, both being subject to secure accommodation proceedings. Of the nine, three young people felt they had been insufficiently prepared in advance. Ten children did not want to go to court at all. There are implications for practice here not only for guardians but also for courts, which tend to be busy places with long waiting periods. It does seem that explaining the process carefully to children and enabling them to visit the courtroom has beneficial effects generally and is very important for some children. The issue reflects the balance between giving importance to children's wishes and feelings (albeit to go to court) and safeguarding their welfare (perhaps protecting them from experiences, processes and emotionally damaging information).

In relation to the final outcome, most children had a good understanding either of the precise nature of the order or of the implications of the order for themselves. Given the significance of court orders in the children's lives, this finding was reassuring.

# CHAPTER 7

# Views about children's solicitors

## RATIONALE

Although children's solicitors were not a specific focus of the research, during the course of the research it became clear that there was an opportunity to evaluate the unique contribution made by children's solicitors, since they work so closely with guardians.

This seemed the more important given discussions about how the service should be developed in future. Currently, in most public law proceedings children have automatic party status and are separately represented by specially qualified solicitors. The guardian on behalf of the child usually instructs the solicitors (unless the child is of sufficient age and understanding to give direct instructions). This is a unique position in English law and is valued by many, but is currently under review.

The aim of this examination was to determine the similarities and differences in the perceived roles of guardians and children's solicitors. In doing this, we sought the views of the guardians, as the professional group most qualified to comment on the contribution, and of other professionals (such as the social workers and other solicitors) and also of the children.

Guardians *ad litem* work in partnership with children's panel solicitors in order to ensure a high standard of legal representation for children. In effect, this often puts the child at an advantage in the legal process, reaffirming the paramountcy principle. In most cases the guardian on behalf of the child instructs the solicitor. As mentioned above the exception to this is where the child can give her/his own instructions. In these circumstances it may be that the young person and guardian are agreed, that is, the child's wishes and feelings are in line with safeguarding the child's interests. If not, the solicitor must take instructions from the young person. It is the child's solicitor's decision whether the young person is of sufficient age or understanding, although the solicitor would take the guardian's view into account.

# PROFESSIONALS' VIEWS OF THE CONTRIBUTION OF CHILDREN'S SOLICITORS

Since guardians and children's solicitors work closely together through-out proceedings, guardians were specifically asked whether they bene-fited from legal representation. The feedback obtained indicated that the majority of the 18 guardians questioned felt that they did benefit from having legal representation.

Only two guardians reported that they had not benefited from legal representation. These guardians commented that this was due to the solic-itors having limited involvement with their cases. The comments were as follows:

*Solicitor was far too busy dashing off here and there.*

*Due to time constraints there was limited liaison with child's solicitor.*

The remaining 16 guardians reported that they had benefited from legal representation. These guardians identified a number of advantages of having their own legal representation. Firstly, guardians valued guidance on legal issues, particularly in complex cases. Guardians recognised the benefit of having a person skilled in presenting an articulate legal argu-ment. Guardians benefited from the advocacy skills of children's solici-tors (as did the children). These skills were particularly valuable when guardians and children had different views and separated. Guardians reported that solicitors were supportive and allowed them to discuss issues and concerns. The extensive knowledge of children's solicitors on previous proceedings was also of benefit to guardians. Finally, guardians reported that they benefited from solicitors' influence over the local authority. The comments were as follows:

[Benefited] *from having someone articulate to put forward the legal case.*

*Legal advice sought readily available with full insight of case. Sought purely from child's perspective. Excellent.*

[Benefited from] *advocacy skills in court on behalf of child where there was some potential her needs/rights could be compromised otherwise.*

[Benefited from] *having someone equally committed to promoting the children's interests with whom I could discuss issues and concerns.*

*The legal representative had known the young person from past dealings and worked in partnership with the guardian.*

*Reinforced message to local authority to explore placement issues in more depth by using her role directly with local authority legal representative.*

Other professionals are unlikely to be aware of the discussions between guardians and solicitors during the process of proceedings; legal advice given; the value of the partnership in teasing out issues and focusing the work; or of how this contributes to the planning and assessment. Nevertheless, some professionals did perceive the benefit of legal representation for guardians and children.

Out of the 64 non-guardians who responded to the questionnaire, 24 (37.5%) rated children's solicitors as contributing 'a little' to the case and 39 (60.9%) rated them as contributing 'quite a lot' or 'very much'. One respondent did not provide a rating. These figures include the self-ratings of 20 children's solicitors. By excluding these self-ratings we find similar percentages for each category: unanswered at 1.9% (1/51); 'a little' at 35.3% (18/51); and 'quite a lot' with 'very much' at 62.7% (32/51). Thus, the findings shown above are not markedly skewed by the self-reports of children's solicitors. Because of this, ratings from all non-guardians will be presented together.

Twenty-four non-guardians rated the contribution of the children's solicitors as 'a little'. They included six from social workers, seven from local authority solicitors, five from parents' solicitors and six from children's solicitors. The ratings related to 14 cases.

Professionals provided few comments with ratings. The comments available reveal some reasons why the contribution of the children's solicitors was minimal: (1) a case was inevitable; (2) guardian practice was of a high standard; and (3) the children's solicitor had no contact with her client. For example:

*Quality of guardian's work resulted in lesser input being required to safeguard the interests of the child.*          (Children's solicitor)

Comments revealed that children's solicitors made a contribution from their knowledge of a case, their ability to obtain official documents and their liaison with the local authority. The comments were as follows:

*The fact that the guardian and the child's legal representative already*

*had knowledge and experience of the family and previous
proceedings was helpful.* (Social worker)

*Child's legal representative obtained a copy of the paper from the
case in which the mother's partner was convicted of a Schedule 1
offence. Those papers helped the mother in making the decision to
separate from her partner.* (Local authority solicitors)

The majority (60.9%) of professionals rated children's solicitors as
having made 'quite a lot' or 'very much' of a contribution to proceedings.
Thirteen (65%) social workers provided these ratings as well as 7 (50%)
local authority solicitors, 12 (71%) parents' solicitors and 7 (54%) children's solicitors.

Comments revealed a range of ways in which the children's solicitor
made a substantial contribution to a case. Their contribution came in
cases where the guardian and young person had different views and also
in complex cases. Professionals noted that children's solicitors made a
contribution by obtaining the wishes of children, in order to safeguard
their interests. Children's solicitors explained the legal position to children. They were also helpful in focusing the local authority on important
issues and were seen as helpful and experienced practitioners.

For example, in relation to the guardian and children having different
views:

*Absolutely essential that the child had own legal representative in
view of age, issues of restraining liberty in conflict with guardian.*
(Children's solicitor)

The children's solicitor was seen as being helpful in complex cases:

*This case was not straightforward and it was clear that the views of
the guardian should equally be presented by an able and experienced
advocate.* (Parent's solicitor)

On occasion the children's solicitor obtained the wishes and feelings of
the child or safeguarded the interests of children:

*It was extraordinarily useful to the court for the children's position
and perspective to be investigated and presented with clarity and
complete independence by the guardian and the child's solicitor.*
(Parent's solicitor)

Sometimes the children's solicitor was helpful in explaining the legal
position with children:

*By discussing with young person the reasons for the local authority's applications and the serious nature of the concerns.* (Social worker)

Or in helping the local authority to focus on important issues:

*At points seemed the most experienced practitioner and focused minds on real points of issue.* (Parent's solicitor)

Children's solicitors were also seen as helpful and experienced practitioners:

*Mother was represented by solicitor who was not proficient in family proceedings ... This led to excessive use of court time ... The solicitor representing the child worked very hard to address issues when inappropriately addressed.* (Social worker)

## CONCLUSION (REGARDING THE CONTRIBUTION OF CHILDREN'S LEGAL REPRESENTATIVE)

Professionals identified some common areas in which guardians and children's solicitors made a contribution to proceedings. Guardians and children's solicitors both assist the local authority to focus on important issues. Both obtain the wishes and feelings of the child, although for younger children the guardian's special skills may be necessary. They often have an extensive knowledge of previous proceedings. One can deduce that these shared roles of guardians and children's solicitors facilitate movement of proceedings towards a less contentious and more child-focused conclusion.

Professionals identified a number of unique ways in which children's solicitors contribute to proceedings. Foremost, children's solicitors provide legal advice and explain the legal position to children thoroughly and thoughtfully. Children's solicitors use their advocacy skills on behalf of children. They are also able to obtain official documents. Guardians do not have the necessary skills or training to perform adequately the present duties of children's solicitors. This suggests a need to have both a guardian and a children's solicitor to represent children throughout proceedings, in order to ensure that children continue to receive a high standard of representation in court. The importance of having a children's solicitor is highlighted in situations where the guardian and young person have different views on what is best for the young person.

Throughout this report children's solicitors and guardians identified a number of benefits of having a working partnership. The supportive relationship between children's solicitors and guardians enables them to fulfil their common aim of obtaining the wishes and feelings of children while safeguarding the interests of children, and as such is clearly valued by both.

## CHILDREN'S VIEWS OF THEIR SOLICITOR

Nine children could not remember meeting their solicitor at any time during the proceedings. The guardians of five of these children (aged between 8 and 11 years) confirmed that the children had not had any contact with their solicitor. Three guardians provided explanations of why the children did not meet their solicitor.

*The children had seen too many professionals during the course of the court case – police, counsellors, psychologist, etc.*

*I [guardian] liaised with social services, psychologists and we all felt there were enough different adults involved in her life and my involvement was kept low-profile anyway; we considered it would not have helped her to meet her solicitor, of whom she would have had little understanding.*

*Child didn't have a solicitor (Legal Aid are no longer funding in these circumstances).*

At no point during the interview did the children who did not meet their solicitor talk about the solicitor's role.

The guardian of one 9-year-old girl stated that she met her solicitor during the previous proceedings but not in the current proceedings. No explanation was given for not arranging a meeting between the solicitor and the girl in the more recent proceedings.

Two children stated that their solicitor had visited them when their guardian reported that they had not. One girl had been visited by her solicitor in previous proceedings, which could account for her response. In total, seven children did not receive a visit from their solicitor, according to guardians.

There were four children aged between 8 and 12 years who, according to their guardian, met their solicitor but could not recall doing so. The guardians of two of these children reported their solicitor had met the children once only. One 11-year-old had reportedly seen his solicitor once and also at court.

One child met his solicitor two or three times before the guardian was appointed because there was a waiting list for guardians as the number of referrals into the panel exceeded the number of guardians available for work. It is not surprising that this 8-year-old could not remember meeting his solicitor some 6 months prior to the research interview.

Seventeen children could recall meeting their solicitor. Most ($N = 10$) children saw their solicitor twice. Three met their solicitor once only. Three saw their solicitor three times and one young person saw her solicitor around 15 times.

The majority ($N = 16$) of solicitors visited children with the guardian for at least their first visit. Max was the only child who had received his only visit from his solicitor without his guardian being present.

Alice (11 years), Chantelle (15 years), Claire (13 years) and Ryan (14 years) could recall their solicitor's full name. Three of these young people saw their solicitor twice and Chantelle saw her solicitor around 15 times. Twelve-year-old Sarah remembered her solicitor's first name only. None of the remaining twelve children could recall their solicitor's name but claimed to recognise it when prompted.

> I can't remember her name now, that other woman [solicitor]. She came with [guardian] one time. I can't remember her name though.
>
> (Matthew, 13 years)

The solicitors' visits were seen by some children as happy events involving outings, usually with the guardian, to restaurants. Chantelle (15 years) saw her solicitor:

> About 15 or something, 15 times. More than my guardian because she was my solicitor. We went to Burger King. She used to write things down what I'd say but that's normal.
>
> [Solicitor] was with [guardian] cause twice I've seen her and [guardian] took us to McDonalds with her a couple of times.   (Louise, 11 years)

For others the solicitor's visits involved the solicitor introducing her/himself and explaining her/his role. The visits did not involve a lot of talking by either the solicitor or young person.

> [Guardian's] friend [solicitor], her friend who came to see us when the guardian first came to speak to us as well. I can't remember her friend's name ... [Guardian's] friend just says what her job is and what her name is and then left ... [Talked to solicitor] only a bit but then I weren't really bothered because I liked it more talking to [guardian] because I knew her more because she came around more and I only wanted to talk to one person because it was easier.
>
> (Caroline, 10 years)

[Solicitor] *was just introducing herself to me and that. She said my proper solicitor can't represent me because she is for Crown Court and this is Family Court.* [She didn't really talk much about what I wanted.] *She read a lot about me. She was arguing up for me. She thought I was ready to go home but the court didn't.* (John, 12 years)

Courtney and Jamie Lee remembered their solicitor explaining what they were going to do in court for them.

[Solicitor] *just told us what she was going to do for us and what her job was and stuff like that. Her job was to find out what we wanted so that she could pass it on at court.* (Jamie Lee, 15 years)

[Solicitor] *just talked to us about what she was going to do at court.* (Courtney, 11 years)

Ryan and Claire's solicitors saw them for about an hour, in which time their solicitors answered questions and discussed what Ryan and Claire wanted.

[Solicitor] *was alright. They* [guardian and solicitor] *used to talk about me behind my back though.* [Saw solicitor] *once, that was when I was in court I think ... told her what I wanted and everything so I got about an hour, before I went in* [to courtroom]. (Claire, 13 years)

[Saw solicitor] *before I went to court and then when I was at court – twice. I think she came once with* [guardian]. *She asked a few questions, asked me my name and stuff like that.* [Spent] *about an hour or something.* (Ryan, 14 years)

Thirteen-year-old Matthew talked to his solicitor 'about what I wanted and who I wanted to live with.'

As mentioned earlier, eight children saw the solicitor as someone whom their guardian spoke to about them.

[Guardian spoke to] *the woman that she brought with her that was the lawyer but I didn't know her.* (Jamie Lee, 15 years)

[Guardian] *just says like I'm going to talk to* [solicitor]. (Chantelle, 15 years)

Some children knew that their guardian needed to talk to their solicitor about what they wanted so that the court could be informed in turn.

[Guardian would say to the court] *'these* [siblings] *want to go back to*

*their mum'. But she'd not actually tell them herself because that's
what the solicitor is for.*                     (Jamie Lee, 15 years)

[Guardian] *told* [solicitor] *first and then they told court together I
think.*                                         (Sarah, 12 years)

The solicitor for two children explained to them what the guardian's
role was.

[Solicitor] *just says what their* [guardian and solicitor's] *jobs are, same
as* [guardian] *did.*                           (Caroline, 10 years)

The solicitors of three children joined guardians in their good-bye visit.
They helped to explain to children what the court had decided should
happen to them.

*I met my solicitor twice. Once when the World Cup had just started
and the last day* [my guardian] *came to see me.*        (Josh, 8 years)

Claire, who was 13 years old, saw her solicitor as someone who
stopped her from going to her final hearing.

*My solicitor and* [guardian] *... wouldn't let me go* [to final hearing],
*they just said it was best not to.*

There were 17 cases where the child concerned clearly remembered
seeing his or her solicitor. The overall impression is that, for the individual
children, the solicitors had some significance but the degree of this
varied.

## CONCLUSION

The solicitors had far less significance for children than for the guardian,
and even this limited significance did not remain beyond the proceedings,
with the solicitor fading from memory. Only five young people knew the
solicitor's name, either in full or in part, at the time the research was
undertaken; these young people were all aged over 11 years. We would
refer again to the sub-conclusion above, concerning how solicitors and
guardians value their working partnership and the benefit they believe
this brings to both assessing the wishes and feelings of children and to
safeguarding their interests.

# CHAPTER 8

# Discussion of the research findings

These two research studies have complemented each other and explored different aspects of a complex process.

## THE VIEWS OF PROFESSIONALS

The research into professionals' views aimed to explore what contribution guardians make throughout the course of public family law proceedings and to the outcome. We wanted to establish what aspects of the guardian's role are seen to be effective and of particular added value to professionals involved in proceedings. There were a number of key findings, some expected and some unexpected; some of these will now be discussed in turn.

### THE GUARDIAN'S CONTRIBUTION THROUGHOUT THE COURSE OF PROCEEDINGS

The research revealed a number of ways in which guardians influence the process of proceedings. One way in which guardians were seen to do this was by working closely with social workers to assist in the formulation of a comprehensive care plan. In particular guardians influenced change in the final care plan by providing information on the needs of children and their carers and in some cases assisted social workers by initiating expert assessments.

The study also found that in most agreed cases guardians were seen by all the professionals concerned as contributing, often significantly, towards the agreement. Their contribution came from their involvement with parents and the local authority, and in commissioning expert assessments throughout the course of proceedings. The independence of guardians allowed them to act as mediators when there were 'sticking points'. Parents responded positively to guardians spending time listening to them and sharing investigation findings, often helping them to move towards agreement.

Professionals reported that guardians also made a substantial contribution to proceedings by revealing new pieces of information and bringing new issues to the attention of other professionals. For example, guardians were in a unique position to raise information on the views of parents, the criminal history of parents and medical evidence. They also addressed issues around the situation of extended family members, the inappropriateness of care plan recommendations and the need for specialist work with children.

Thus by influencing the care plan, working with parents and the local authority towards an agreed outcome, and revealing new information and issues guardians contributed to the process of proceedings. Professionals saw these aspects of the guardian's role as adding value to proceedings.

## THE GUARDIAN'S CONTRIBUTION TOWARDS THE OUTCOME

The professionals' research revealed that guardians not only make a valuable contribution throughout proceedings but also can in some cases influence the type of order made. While the findings showed that the impact of the guardian is less significant where the outcome is clear-cut and where social services input was of a high standard, it follows that impact is likely to be greatest where issues are contested. Professionals identified that in 15 out of 21 cases a different outcome would have been reached if a guardian had not been involved. Comments from these professionals illustrated that the positive influence of the guardian particularly came from their independent position so that the guardian's view added weight to or confirmed the social worker view. However the comments revealed that the presence of a guardian not only affected the type of order made in some proceedings, but also whether an order was reached with agreement or conflict between parties and with or without delay. Similarly, in cases where professionals considered that the same outcome would have been achieved without a guardian they considered that the proceedings would have been longer and more contentious.

## THE ADDED VALUE OF GUARDIANS

Professionals identified a number of aspects of the guardian's role that were of particular added value to proceedings. Professionals particularly valued the guardian's role of expressing the wishes and feelings of children, thus keeping the focus on children throughout proceedings. They also valued the guardian's role of explaining the court process to children. Guardians provided an independent view of a case, which facilitated settlement, as discussed above. Professionals valued the guardian's role of providing a thorough investigation of a case, revealing new pieces of information and issues along the way. In the process the guardian encourages the local authority to keep the salient issues to the fore. Thus the added presence of a guardian can make some proceedings less contentious, shorter, more comprehensive and more child-focused.

Overall, the research among professionals illustrated the influence the guardian has on the course of proceedings, that is, the process. While this may not manifest itself in changes to actual outcome, it adds a number of perspectives. This contribution encompasses negotiating, investigating, explaining, sharing information (openness), focusing on key issues and enhancing co-operation. A very significant finding is the value (by all concerned) of the independence of guardians. One direct effect is to lessen contentiousness, with the result that applications or opposition to applications altered. A consistent finding of the research on professionals' views was that guardians made a major contribution through being child-focused, keeping individual children's wishes and feelings to the fore, and explaining processes to the children.

Greater emphasis is given here to discussion of the research on children's views, as the points made above are explored in more detail in Chapter 2 and 3.

## THE VIEWS OF CHILDREN

The aim of this research was by definition more child-focused, concentrating on children's perspectives and understanding. Again some of the findings were in line with expectations and others were unexpected. The findings also demonstrated the variations in individual guardians' practice. What was surprising for the researcher was the depth of knowledge that some children had, their grasp of the issues and the sophistication of their understanding.

### CHILDREN'S UNDERSTANDING OF THE ROLE OF THE GUARDIAN

The 28 children we interviewed were of various ages, between 8 and 15 years. It was encouraging to find that half of these children had a comprehensive understanding of the guardian service, recognising that a guardian's job is to establish a child's wishes and feelings and represent these in court. Some, however, had a much more limited understanding. For most children the guardian was the only person who explained to them what their role was, although five children said the social worker had described the role to them. Thus guardians have a crucial role in preparing children for being the subject of court processes and the people they may subsequently meet. Training for social workers on the role of the guardian would be advantageous, so that they might also prepare the children. It follows that guardians should ascertain what social workers have and have not told children about their involvement in proceedings in order to ensure that children are adequately informed about the court process.

That some children had a confused understanding of the guardian service is illustrated in the range of responses obtained from children when answering the question about whom the guardian worked for, with the majority of children unaware that guardians were associated with the court or (locally) The Children's Society. Of particular concern were the children who associated their guardian with social services. It is in the best interests of children for them to be aware of a guardian's independent role in order that they may have the opportunity to relate to and speak to the guardian without prejudice and free of expectations towards the local authority (Kerr and Gregory, 1998). Their understanding of the guardian service was, however, different from their understanding of the guardian's task, but we note that this also needed clarification in some cases.

## INFORMING CHILDREN

This research indicates that guardians need to be clearer with children in respect of their independent role, and this issue may need to be repeated by guardians (and indeed others, e.g. solicitors and carers) throughout proceedings in order to ensure that children retain this information.

Information leaflets on the guardian service appear to be under-utilised by guardians with the children we interviewed, as only ten children could recall receiving a leaflet. Reasons given by guardians for not using leaflets are varied, including the view that the available leaflets are not age-appropriate to younger children. Some of the concerns are echoed in the study by Masson and Winn Oakley (1999), and new leaflets may need to be developed by the guardian service for all panels. Ideally leaflets need to be appropriate for children over a wide age range, should be clear, informative and comprehensive, and have an appropriate balance between children's rights and their welfare.

The benefits of providing children with information leaflets need to be explored with guardians. Information leaflets can be an effective tool for explaining the guardian service, and can be referred back to by children on their own or with their guardian in order to clarify issues around the guardian's role, the solicitor's role and the court process. If adequate leaflets are available best practice might have the guardian take a child through the leaflet at the first visit and perhaps periodically throughout proceedings with the aim of giving children a clear and comprehensive understanding of the service. Children and their carers could then refer back to this information throughout proceedings.

Another valuable tool for explaining the role of the guardian (and that of other professionals) is the 'Not alone' video and accompanying colouring book produced by the Department of Health, which is appropriate for younger children aged between 8 and 12 years and can be watched with the guardian present or left with children to view at their leisure, for discussion at a subsequent visit.

### LISTENING TO CHILDREN AND ESTABLISHING WISHES AND FEELINGS

According to the children we interviewed the most important characteristic of a guardian is their ability to listen to children and explain things to them. This is only one part of a guardian's role but a significant and highly valued part, since guardians cannot perform their duties adequately if they have not obtained an accurate picture of a child's wishes and feelings. The majority of guardians appeared to match children's expectations and many children cited a number of reasons for feeling listened to. Their guardian may have answered their questions, written down what they had said or merely looked at them while they were talking. The children showed enthusiasm and surprise at being listened to and clearly valued this experience. For some children the guardian seemed to be the first person who had really listened to them and sought their opinion, which may account for one boy's decision to test out his guardian to see if he was really being listened to.

In contrast to this there were three young people, each with a different guardian, who did not feel sufficiently listened to. Two young people were living in secure and residential units and believed that their guardians listened only some of the time to them. All three reported that their guardians listened to their sibling, social worker or the radio, respectively, instead of listening to them.

It is vital that the guardian hears correctly what children want given the duty to convey the wishes and feelings of a child to the court. Most children thought that their guardian understood where they wanted or did not want to live and/or whom they wanted or did not want to see, including the one boy who had said his guardian had not listened to him as she listened to the radio instead.

Four children thought that their guardian had not sufficiently understood what they wanted to happen to them and, not surprisingly, two of these young people had reported that their guardian had not listened to them either. Throughout the interview these two young people expressed feelings of frustration and anger at their guardian for not fully comprehending their wishes and feelings. These feelings may have been exacerbated by their isolation at living in residential and secure units. However, the anger and frustration shown by one of these young people is understandable considering her report that her guardian told her father something that she had specifically asked her not to repeat to him. This highlights the need for guardians to make clear that information cannot be kept confidential from the court and others involved, for example parents. Also guardians need to work closely and openly with these isolated young people in order to gain their trust and co-operation, and perhaps need to be clearer about the dual role of assessing wishes and feelings and also best interests (see below).

The two children who felt that their guardian listened to what they were saying but did not understand the significance of their statements highlight the distinction between being listened to and being heard. One reason for this lack of understanding may have been that these children found it difficult to express themselves adequately, but this is where the guardian's skills in communication should come into play. Guardians need to regularly check with children that they have understood their meaning correctly.

### CONVEYING WISHES AND FEELINGS TO THE COURT

It was concerning that two children were unaware of one of the main duties of their guardian, that of conveying their wishes and feelings to the court. However, most children knew that their guardian conveyed what they wanted to the court and had a good understanding of how they did this. The children were aware that their guardian talked to the judge or magistrates, wrote to the court, or passed a message to the court through the solicitor. Overall it appears that guardians are skilled at explaining to children how decisions are made and the weight given by the court to the children's wishes and feelings. Unfortunately this good practice did not extend to the guardians of four children who did not know how their guardian informed the court of where they wanted to live and/or whom they wanted to see. Two of these children reported that they did not know this because they had not gone to court. Whether or not children go to court, they should be aware of the process by which the guardian conveys their wishes and feelings to the court. Guardians may consider (if they do not do so already) assisting children to write a letter to the judge or magistrates, for incorporation in their report. Showing children the Welfare Checklist (see S1(3) of the Children Act 1989) could be a way of helping children to understand the complexity of decision-making, and it would follow from this that the guardian explained how she/he would inform the court of wishes and feelings. These practices might help children to be reassured that their views are being heard and considered by the court.

Most children believed that their guardian knew them well enough to inform the court of their wishes and feelings in a report. There was a link between feeling understood and being confident that the guardian could write an appropriate report to the court. However, one young person did not feel sufficiently understood to be confident that the guardian could reflect his wishes and feelings accurately, thus highlighting the importance of guardians checking with children that they have understood their wishes and feelings to their satisfaction. This appears to have been done by the guardian of one other young person who believed that her guardian could write an adequate report despite feeling that she did not fully understand her reasons for not wanting to live with her mother. At least this young person had some confidence that her guardian understood the fundamental issue of where she wanted to live.

Two young people felt both that their guardian did not understand what they wanted and would not be able to adequately state this in a report. These two young people, who lived in secure and residential units, thought that their guardians did not know them well enough because they had not spent enough time with them. One young person also reported feeling restricted in what she could tell her guardian owing to the presence of her step-father during visits, reflecting the importance of seeing children on their own even when matters seem straightforward. The Humberside Panel has drawn up guidelines for working with children to ensure their safety as well as ensuring that they feel listened to. These guidelines were produced because of a general awareness that professionals sometimes abuse children, but there was a consensus view that children should have the opportunity to talk to guardians on their own, it being an expectation of the court that this will have happened. Guardians are aware that even to use a separate room in a house where children do not feel safe is not sufficient. On other occasions there may be good reason not to take a child out. It remains a matter of judgement for the individual guardian, but hopefully the comments made in this research will highlight the need to ensure children feel they have had sufficient opportunity to talk and have been listened to.

Guardians are in a difficult position of balancing children's rights to know how a guardian is representing their views to the court and protecting them from potentially damaging information about their parents and life history. One 15-year-old provided a striking illustration of why guardians must take care when showing young people their report. (Chantelle, who commented that while 'it was right', she 'didn't want to hear them kind of things'). This may account for the relatively small number of children who could remember being shown or described parts of the guardian's report. In order to attain the right balance it may be advisable for guardians to show children the wishes and feelings section of their report or at least describe this section to them in an age-appropriate manner using a variety of techniques. This would allow children to check that guardians are representing their wishes and feelings correctly to the court. Bearing in mind the time constraints one suggestion is to write this section of the report in advance. In secure accommodation proceedings it could even be done, perhaps in annotated form, while with the young person. This would prevent young people like Matthew, John and Claire feeling that guardians have not understood them and/or that they have been misrepresented to the court. A further suggestion is to follow the practice of some guardians and help the child write a book (e.g. a school exercise book) about themselves and some of the aspects of their lives about which they have strong feelings.

## INTERVIEWING OTHERS

Most of the children we interviewed were aware of the guardian's duty to contact significant people in their lives in order to develop a comprehensive understanding of them, but they were unsure about who their guardian actually spoke to. Guardians need to inform the child that they will be contacting teachers, other professionals and family members. Notably guardians reported speaking to the teachers of 14 children whereas none of these children reported being aware of this. The trust and respect of children towards their guardian may be eroded once they discover that their guardian has talked to someone without their prior knowledge.

An issue may arise if a child has reservations about the guardian seeing a specific person. Again, the child may need to be helped to understand that the guardian has a range of specific duties, of which understanding the child's wishes and feelings is only one. Guardians are there to investigate matters on behalf of the court and to share information they obtain with the court. Therefore there is a tension, potentially, between their different roles. The guardian, as investigator, cannot give promises of confidentiality to anyone they interview, including the child. The child could be given the opportunity to identify alternative people, but if this is not appropriate guardians should explain to children why it is necessary for them to go ahead with their visit. It is especially important in these situations to keep children informed of when a visit has been scheduled and once again when the visit has taken place in order to keep proceedings open to children. We consider that best practice would be for guardians to discuss with children who they see and keep them regularly informed of whom they intend to see and whom they have seen. In general children benefit from being well informed, having their opinions valued and making a contribution to proceedings.

## BALANCING WISHES AND FEELINGS WITH SAFEGUARDING INTERESTS

The majority of guardians communicated clearly to children their reasons why they could or could not support children's wishes in their recommendations to the court. Children of varying ages recognised that their guardian agreed with what they wanted because it was in their best interests. The guardians of five children illustrated good practice in acknowledging children's wishes and feelings whilst communicating to them that in their view what they wanted was not in their best interests and forewarning them that their wishes may not come true in court. However, this good practice was overshadowed by the experience of eight children who either could not remember their guardian telling them whether they agreed or disagreed with their wishes, or mistakenly believed that their guardian disagreed with them. The guardians' questionnaire revealed that the guardians of half of these children agreed that what they wanted was in their best interests and would be recommended to the court. The guardians of these children did not make their agreement clear, yet it may have helped to allay some of the children's apprehensions about the proceedings to know that their guardian fully supported their views on what should happen to them. Two guardians encountered difficulties in clearly explaining to two boys with learning difficulties that they could not support their wishes to live back at home. These findings highlight the need for guardians to find other methods of communication to reinforce information for children, particularly those with learning difficulties. Showing children the Welfare Checklist could be a way for guardians to help children understand their duty to assess best interests and how these may be safeguarded, leading to a discussion of what recommendations they will be making to the court. Guardians need to reiterate information to children until they have a clear understanding of their guardian's recommendations to the court and the reasons behind their decision.

It was interesting to find that most children felt listened to and understood even when their wishes were not followed. This demonstrates that children have sophisticated thinking whereby they can acknowledge the good work done by guardians despite not getting what they want. Some children do have an understanding that their best interests may not be served by what they ideally want. Alternatively children may not expect their wishes and feelings to be acted upon, depending on what they want.

## THE PATTERN OF VISITING

The majority of children were happy with the timing of guardians' visits and were forewarned of their intended visit by people who were living with them or by their guardian. Writing letters to children and scheduling appointments at the end of visits appeared to be effective ways for guardians to prepare children for their visits. The children who were unhappy with the timing of their guardian's visits and not prepared for visits contrasted with this good practice. Notably two of these children were in a secure or residential unit where it is at the discretion of staff to inform children of visits and decide when visits should take place. Staff may not always forward letters on to young people in secure accommodation, as was the researcher's experience with letters written to a boy in a secure unit. Guardians may need to find alternative means to inform young people of when and why they intend to visit them, for example following up a letter with a phone call.

For guardians there will always be a tension in developing a relationship with a child owing to the finite nature of their involvement, especially when there are changes in social worker, a sporadic social work involvement and when a child needs continuity and contact. Fortunately the children we interviewed were clear that the reason their guardian came to visit them was to find out who they wanted to live with and/or see. In addition, some children related this to the guardian's role of informing the court of what they wanted. Guardians need to be clear with themselves and children the purpose of each visit and have a clear agenda to ascertain specific information on the wishes and feelings of children. In general visits that serve only to develop or maintain the relationship with a child are not helpful to either the guardian or child (unless this is itself a specific purpose, e.g. when there are long delays).

## THE INVOLVEMENT OF THE SOLICITOR

Out of the 28 children, seven had no contact with a solicitor, but of these one was not represented, Legal Aid not being available. The research showed that unless the children actually met their solicitor, this person/role had no relevance for them.

Seventeen children had a clear recollection of meeting their solicitor, most seeing the solicitor twice. Usually the guardian introduced the solicitor to the child, which seems appropriate, but there were occasions when the solicitor saw the child alone at least once. This reflects the solicitor's duty to decide whether the child is able to give direct instructions. It is not clear from the research whether the children understood the different roles of the solicitor and guardian. Only a small number of children aged between 11 and 14 (five in all) could remember their solicitor's name.

For those 17 children who remembered their solicitor's visit the solicitors had some significance but the degree of this varied with the nature of the visits, from social outings to restaurants accompanied by guardians to discussions on what the children wanted and/or the role of professionals. Some children recalled their solicitor explaining their role, particularly about court or the guardian's role. A few children were aware that their guardian needed to talk to their solicitor about what they wanted in order to inform the court. Some solicitors also helped to explain to children the court's decision during the guardian's good-bye visit.

One suggestion for future practice is that the guardian and solicitor together arrange for the child to see the court building and explain who sits where and what everyone in court does, so that the child's understanding of the solicitor's role is enhanced by being able to visualise them in the court context.

## CHILDREN'S ATTENDANCE AT COURT

Only 15 of the 28 children wanted to attend court or see the courtroom, and of these only nine did so. Two of these children were subject to secure accommodation applications and so their attendance was a requirement. Consequently there were 13 children subject to care or related proceedings who wanted either involvement in the court hearing or an understanding of the process (seeing the courtroom, hearing where people sat, meeting the judge or magistrates, etc.).

The research indicated that some children were dissuaded from attending court, despite their wish to do so, and of these some were not given the opportunity even to see the courtroom. Given a presumption that they may attend (and indeed their presence should be formally excused), further research may be needed to ascertain whether this Humberside pattern reflects a nationwide trend.

The six children who wanted to go to court and did not were reportedly not allowed to go because their guardian said they were 'too young'. Despite being 'too young' the children who did not attend court had clear reasons why they needed and wanted to go, including seeing for themselves what the court did. We would suggest guardians should try to carry out children's wishes as closely as possible, within reason. One young person wanted to have more of an involvement by attending the final hearing in addition to the directions hearing she went to. This young person wanted to go to the final hearing to be told directly the reasons why the case was withdrawn, as she did not believe the account given by her guardian and social worker in a letter, emphasising how some children have a greater need to be involved in the process.

Another boy wanted to tell the court in his own words what he wanted. For this child a visit to an empty courtroom may not have met his needs, whereas the opportunity to speak to the magistrates may have done. His guardian could have assisted the boy to write a letter to the court that might well have helped him to feel that the magistrates listened directly to him.

Inevitably children's views of court are influenced by what they see on television, which is rarely representative of what actually happens in public family law proceedings, not only because things happen less quickly there than in a televised presentation of court. It is therefore reassuring to find that six of the nine children who attended court were prepared in advance for their visit by their guardian, foster carer or friend who had previous experience of the Family Court. It was unfortunate that three young people were not prepared for their visit to the court, particularly two young people who were present at court hearings. It would seem essential that young people such as these should be prepared in some detail about the set-up and complexity of court proceedings before attending any hearings.

We should also be mindful of the report of one young person who with hindsight was glad she had not gone to court because her sibling who went did not have a good experience after hearing evidence about her parents. This report highlights the need to balance children's rights to information and their rights to protection. We would suggest that the next best alternative to attending a hearing is to show children the empty courtroom. Most courts now make a provision for guardians to do this at the end of the afternoon to coincide with children's availability after school. This enables children to get a sense of where their parents, social worker, guardian, solicitor and judge/magistrates will be sitting. It provides an opportunity to explain further the court process, including how everyone gets to express their point of view including the guardian and children's solicitor on their behalf and how it is the judge's or magistrates' decision as to what should happen to them. It is a way of helping children understand and visualise what the process will be, and why it is not a good idea to be at the hearing (if indeed it is not). It is about children understanding, so feeling they can contribute without having responsibility for the decision-making. If children understand the process and have confidence that their guardian and solicitor understand their position and can reflect their point of view and their need for protection, then this should help. With potential benefits for children one must ask why six children in our sample who wanted to attend court were not given an opportunity to at least see the courtroom.

If more children are to attend court this would have major implications to the court set-up including the environment and timing of hearings. The waiting area for children would need to be child-friendly, appropriately supervised and away from adults subject to criminal proceedings. Hearings would need to be run with minimal delay to save children from added anxiety. Judges and magistrates would need to be prepared for meeting children. These proposed changes to the court culture require co-operation and commitment from all parties to proceedings, particularly court personnel. Above all we must remember to ascertain how children want to be involved in the court process. Some children would not be comfortable attending a court hearing. In fact ten children in our study did not want to go to court after being informed what court was like. These children were able to make an informed decision with the assistance of their guardians and were all happy with hindsight with their decision.

## CHILDREN'S PERCEPTION OF THE OUTCOME

Since only two children were in court when the decision was given, the task of informing children of the court's decision was largely undertaken by the guardian and social worker, but not necessarily together at the same time. One young person who heard the magistrates' decision in court did not understand what was said and needed clarification from the social worker and child's solicitor, illustrating the need to make children's involvement in the court process more meaningful.

Children's understanding of the court's decision ranged widely but those with a limited understanding at least knew that the court had decided where they should live and whom they could see. Encouragingly some children, both younger and older, were aware of the terms of the court orders made; for example, a few children on care orders knew that at age 16 they could move out of foster care if they wished. In addition some children were aware of the reasons why the magistrates or judge made an order and under what circumstances the order would be changed. Thus, overall, the children we interviewed appeared to have a good understanding of the court's decision reflecting the work of guardians and social workers.

Of the children who were asked for their response to the court's decision around half were happy with the outcome as it complied with what they had wanted throughout the course of proceedings. Sadly one young person had been placed on a care order as she wished (above all she wanted to live with her siblings) but the care plan was not followed and she was still living with her parents at the time of the research interview while her siblings remained in foster care. This is an illustration of how actual outcomes may not match plans, nor follow wishes and feelings. Further research is needed on outcomes and their effects on future decision-making, but this is beyond the scope of this research.

The remaining ten children reported that the outcome of their court case was not what they had wanted, with most wanting to go home to their parent/s or to a children's home but were placed instead in a secure unit, residential unit or foster home. It would be interesting to explore how this influenced outcomes after the final hearing as the court's decision is just one outcome in the proceedings. Another might be, for example, the effect on the success of foster placement when an order is made against the child's wishes. We would suggest that future studies incorporate a follow-up study of outcomes.

Unfortunately in some cases the court's decision would never be able to live up to children's wishes as it is not always possible to return children to their family home or to change the circumstances of family members. One girl who knew that her wish to live with both parents would never have been fulfilled as her parents were separated movingly illustrates this. At least this young person was aware of the limitations of the court in changing her family's situation.

## ENDING THE GUARDIAN'S INVOLVEMENT

The good-bye visit provides an opportunity for guardians to explain to children what had happened in court. It is also an opportunity to check out children's understanding of the process of decision-making, the implications for themselves, and the reasons that decisions made may conflict with their own views and feelings. It is an appropriate ending for this stage in the child's life, reinforcing their understanding of the guardian's role being to help the court make decisions, and how these decisions have now been made. We recognise that in some cases a good-bye visit is difficult to make if there is a possibility of future proceedings inevitably involving the same guardian, such as secure accommodation orders, which are renewed every few months. However, young people who are subject to secure orders are old enough to understand that guardian involvement ceases with proceedings. What is important is to emphasise the finite nature of the role.

It was difficult to determine at what point in the proceedings young children were informed that their guardian would stop seeing them after the final hearing since it had already occurred. However, we were able to ascertain that most children were aware of their guardian's limited involvement in proceedings, that is, guardians would make a good-bye visit shortly after the final hearing. Unfortunately, five children were not forewarned of their guardian's final visit and were surprised to learn from their guardian that they would not be returning after the visit. This seems to illustrate that even if guardians do explain in the early stages the limited nature of their role, there is a need to reiterate this at different points in the proceedings. This may become more important in protracted proceedings, when by definition children are seeing their guardian on more occasions.

Of particular concern were the two boys who had a received a good-bye visit from their guardian yet expected to keep seeing their guardian for a number of years after the final hearing. They illustrate why it is so important for guardians to check with children that they have understood the significance of the visit.

Four children did not receive a good-bye visit from their guardian. It appears that the guardian of two girls forgot a promise to return to say a formal farewell after the final hearing. The experience of these girls illustrates that guardians must be clear about what they have promised children. The absence of a proper farewell marred the good work done by the girls' guardian, whom they praised throughout the interview.

One guardian did not make a good-bye visit because of starting leave soon after the final hearing. We would suggest that a visit should have been made when the guardian came back to work, even if this was a number of weeks later, in order to save the child from continuing to wait for their guardian some 4 months after the final hearing. A letter or card in the meanwhile would have helped. It appears that the importance of the good-bye visit needs to be emphasised in terms of normal good practice.

Promisingly, most of the children were clear about the guardian's limited involvement and remembered their good-bye visit vividly taking place on either the day of the final hearing or a few days afterwards. Some guardians chose to mark the occasion by making a special trip with children and sometimes the solicitors to a restaurant or giving the children a small gift. These may be useful ways to emphasise the significance of the good-bye visit, particularly in protracted cases where the guardian has seen a child a number of times.

# KNOWLEDGE GAINED FROM CHILDREN'S RESEARCH METHODOLOGY

In Chapter 1 we discussed the importance of building on the experience of researchers undertaking research with children in order to develop good research practice. In order to add to the collective experience of other researchers we will now present the knowledge that we have gained from undertaking research with children. We hope that this will also assist other researchers, both new and seasoned, in designing methodologically and ethically sound pieces of research.

## INTERVIEW BOARD GAME

Our decision to use the board game with 8- to 11-year-olds appeared to be well founded. However one 12-year-old with mild learning difficulties and one 13-year-old who was anxious about the interview also played the board game and they responded extremely well to the game. A 7-year-old sibling, not included in the research, who used the game did not provide expansive answers to board game questions, indicating that setting a lower age limit of 8 years was appropriate for the content of our questions. That younger and older children responded very well to the board game format suggests that it might be a useful tool for young children through to adolescents, depending on the subject matter to be considered. It is important that children be given a choice of format so that they can decide what best suits their individual needs and competencies.

The children were intrigued to know how the game was played and who had drawn the pictures. The pictures were a topic of discussion and served to help develop a rapport between the interviewer and the children.

The kangaroo hops around questions worked well as all the children appeared to be aware that they had the real option of declining to answer questions they did not wish to answer. In fact one boy stopped at each stop sign to hear what the set of questions coming up were about, thoughtfully considered whether or not he wanted to answer them before stating 'yeah, I'll answer them' or 'yeah, I'll go'. The children felt safe in declining to answer questions as it was incorporated into the game.

The game was a distraction for a few younger children who appeared to be more concerned with finishing the game as quickly as possible by following the kangaroo hops around questions, than actually stopping to talk about their guardian. It may be that for these children they could not remember much about their guardian and that is why they declined to answer most of the questions. It is difficult to know whether these children would have provided more information if another method had been used.

The game was played enthusiastically by most children who focused on the task of answering questions about their guardian. On the whole children provided thoughtful and elaborate answers to questions. Most of the children considered their answers carefully and showed great concern to articulate their thoughts as best they could. Prompts were used to encourage some children to expand on their answers when necessary.

The board game served its purpose of providing a non-threatening means to ask questions in a way that assisted the recall of events.

## WORD AND PHRASE CARD GAME

Results from the word and phrase card game served to reinforce what children had said in the interview. The card game results do not add a great deal of information but they do reveal that we are getting a true picture of children's views. They add validity to the findings of the interview because the children repeated views expressed in the interview.

A strength of the 'ideal' guardian part of the card game was that it differentiated between children who did and did not understand the concept of the game. All but four of the 27 children who completed the task assigned all positive words and phrases to the 'ideal' guardian, with all negative cards placed in the bin. By differentiating between positive and negative these children demonstrate that they understood what was meant by 'ideal' so one could tell whether or not they had known what was meant by an 'ideal' guardian.

A weakness of the card game was that if children appeared not to understand the game (i.e. if they put negative cards into the 'ideal' pile) there was no alternative means for the interviewer of exploring children's views about the 'ideal' guardian. Four children attributed some negative characteristics to an 'ideal' guardian. An 8-year-old and a 10-year-old said that an 'ideal' guardian should be 'difficult to talk to'. A 12-year-old and 14-year-old said that an ideal guardian should be 'too busy to see you'. I checked their answers with these children without highlighting the cards that did not seem to fit. They all confirmed their answers, with one child clarifying that the guardian 'might be' too busy to see children.

## DRAWING/WRITING EXERCISE

The type of feedback received from children through the drawing/writing exercise was not anticipated. The purpose of the exercise had been to give children the opportunity to express memories, feelings and views of their guardian either overlooked or forgotten during the interview. In addition it provided a means for children to express their experience of being in the research. The six children who completed the exercise used it solely to provide feedback on the research and extend their contact with the interviewer. As such, we did not consider the drawing/writing exercise feedback in the findings section. However, the exercise does provide a lot of information on children's experiences of the research process, which will now be examined.

The feedback we received through the drawing/writing exercise illustrated that children wanted to extend their contact with the interviewer. The fact that children knew that the interviewer's involvement was time-limited to one visit only and yet wanted to extend this involvement suggests possible difficulties for guardians owing to the time-limited nature of their work with children. It highlights the need for guardians to mark the end of their involvement with children sensitively and clearly. This issue has previously been discussed in Chapter 5 and earlier in this chapter.

The feedback received from children through the drawing/writing exercise most importantly shows that children enjoyed their experience of meeting the interviewer and being involved in the research.

## WHAT WORKED IN THE INTERVIEWS

We had anticipated that some children would be anxious about being tape-recorded during their interview. However, we found that most of the children were excited to hear themselves on tape and wanted to listen to some or all of the interview. Some children were so excited they asked their foster carer, parent and/or siblings to listen to the tape also. For some children it was the highlight of the interview. It was helpful to give children control over the tape recorder – by giving it to them to hold and turn on and off as they wished. This was done to redress the balance of power between the researcher and the children. The children took their responsibility of controlling the tape recorder seriously.

Asking children to provide a new name for themselves to be used during the interview and on all paperwork served as a valuable tool in three ways. Firstly, it reinforced to the children that their anonymity was assured as their guardian and others would not be able to identify their comments in the report. The children would be able to identify their own comments in the report by remembering their pseudonym. Secondly, it was an icebreaker, with discussions on sport, music and their friends ensuing as they named themselves after footballers, Spice Girls and their friends, etc. Thirdly, the children appeared to enjoy being referred to by their new name throughout the interview.

It was helpful to get younger children to talk about what their guardian looked like and draw a picture of them before the interview began. It served to check whether children were thinking of their guardian and not another professional, such as their social worker or solicitor. Spending time with younger children drawing their guardian served to develop an informal and co-operative relationship between the interviewer and child.

The children were surprised to receive a £5 gift voucher at the end of the interview. The gift vouchers served to show children that their time and views were valued and important, which was regrettably a new concept to some children. We felt it was important to allow children to choose which voucher they received because it reinforced that we recognised and wanted to hear their voice.

## THEMES FROM THE TWO RESEARCH STUDIES

As mentioned at the start of this chapter, the two research studies are complementary, reflecting different aspects of the guardian's involvement, from the perspectives of some, but not all, of those involved. There is coherence in the findings in so far as both research studies highlight the value of the specific focus on children, notably listening to children, explaining the process to them, and explaining their views, wishes and feelings to others, including most importantly the court.

Another consistent finding was concerning the children's solicitors in that they articulate clearly to the court the children's wishes and feelings and explain the legal position and processes. In some circumstances the solicitors are also of central importance in obtaining the young people's wishes and feelings, notably in secure accommodation proceedings, but also occasionally in care or related proceedings.

In terms of the specific focus of the research studies, the research on professionals' views addressed the interface at which the guardians work and the benefits extrapolated from this, particularly the effect on process that itself influences outcomes. The research on children's views reflected the consumer's view, where the consumers (the children) have very little knowledge and understanding of the complexities involved, but they did have a distinct understanding of the parts that were pertinent to them.

## CONCLUSION

The research confirmed the value of guardians to professionals within the court process. Their independence and experience are highly valued, as are the negotiating and mediating skills they bring while continuing to focus on the best interests of the child. The guardian's powers and duties to consider all aspects of the case were seen to put them in an advantageous position when it came to formulating conclusions and recommendations with a view to safeguarding the welfare of children in what were often complex and contentious circumstances.

The research also confirmed the value of the guardian for children, being a service for children in the court setting. We see the two as being inextricably linked.

# CHAPTER 9

# A view to the future: developments in the service for children and the courts

## THE FUTURE

In this final chapter we will discuss future developments of the GALRO service, with the implications from these research findings. Quality assurance is now an important factor for this and other services, and issues of practice are raised, particularly in the research on children's views. We hope that by listening to feedback from these children as well as from professionals, both guardians and those responsible for developing the service will learn and will devise and develop systems for ensuring good practice.

Prior to starting these two research studies, the Department of Health had published *National Standards for the Guardian* ad Litem *and Reporting Officer Service* (Department of Health/Welsh Office, 1995) and had also issued guidance, *Implementing National Standards* in 1996 (Department of Health, 1996). This latter document addresses ways of developing monitoring systems. Court welfare officers, working with families during the course of divorce proceedings, also operate within their own national standards, produced by the Home Office (1994).

During the course of the research, proposals have been made and views sought about the amalgamation of the guardian service with the court welfare service and the children's branch of the official solicitors' department. At the time of going to press, the proposal is to create a Children and Family Court Advisory Service (CAFCAS). Although in the short term it is envisaged that the distinct roles of guardians, court welfare officers and official solicitors will be kept separate, it is anticipated that there will be overlapping functions and over time there may be merging of roles.

The findings in this research combined with other recently published research (e.g. Clark and Sinclair, 1999; Masson and Winn Oakley, 1999) therefore remain pertinent. They also need to be set in the context of studies of family violence and the effect on children (with specific implications for contact orders in private law proceedings), and in the context of the Human Rights Act, to be implemented in October 2000, which requires compatibility with the European Convention for the Protection of Human Rights. Article 3 of the European Convention states:

> In all actions concerning children, whether undertaken by public or private social welfare institutions, Courts of law, administrative authorities or legislative bodies, the best interests of the child shall be the primary consideration.

Similarly Article 12 of the United Nations Convention on the Rights of the Child (1989) states (those concerned) 'shall assure to the child who is capable of forming his or her own views the right to express those views freely in all matters affecting the child, the views of the child being given weight in accordance with the age and maturity of the child'.

The findings of this research illustrate that the high standard of practice of guardians was valued, as was their independent status. What was valued about individual practice was well within national standards, for example highly developed skills in working with children and keeping children informed at a variety of levels (time of appointments, letters to court). Good-bye visits enabled guardians to be very clear about the time-limited nature of their involvement, while making children feel special (Standard 13: 'Prior to closing the case, guardians ensure that they have considered appropriate actions and if necessary carried them out in respect of the child' (Department of Health/Welsh Office, 1995)).

Any shortcomings in individual practice highlighted in the research were in the fine detail of the task undertaken rather than in the parameters. For example, one girl's views were sought but in at least one session she felt unable to express herself fully because her stepfather was present. Standard 5 is that 'Full consideration is given to ascertaining both the wishes and feelings of the child'. Other examples are around children's wish to go to court, 'where the child has sufficient understanding and is able to express her/his wishes and feelings, the guardian should advise about the child's attendance at court'. We would note, however, that the research findings did not reflect a presumption about the child's right to go to court, rather the contrary (i.e. to be protected from having to go to court).

The issue of children's attendance at court could be addressed with both judges and magistrates at Family Court Business Committee meetings locally and nationally at various forums. This, however, is a broader issue than the focus of this research.

## IMPLICATIONS FOR PRACTICE

The findings have highlighted a number of points, both through good practice and, unfortunately, occasional instances of poor practice. If nothing else these latter instances emphasise the importance of monitoring and structured appraisal. We feel these are the key issues to emerge:

### ISSUES FOR GUARDIANS

- *Explaining the task.* For children in this age range it is important for guardians to give their own explanation of what their job entails, and to remind the children of this over time, particularly in protracted proceedings. The use of information leaflets, to accompany verbal explanations, is likely to assist.

- *Explaining independence.* For the children in this study the notion of independence from social services and family seemed to have little relevance. However, it is important and is a concept valued by the adults involved and we feel efforts should be made to help the children understand this, especially as it links with the time-limited nature of the role.

- *Explaining the limits of confidentiality.* Not all the children understood that information they gave to the guardian would be shared with parents and others involved in the court hearing. While being mindful of the conflicts this may create, it is important for guardians to be open and honest about this.

- *Ensuring children are aware about the duty to inform the court of their wishes and feelings.* This central part of the guardian's role was not fully understood by all the children. Suggestions have been made in Chapter 5 about referring to the Welfare Checklist, perhaps even writing section 1(3)(a) – about the child's wishes and feelings – with the child concerned. Our discussions with the children in this study indicate that had this been fully understood, concerns about wanting to speak directly to the judge or magistrates might disappear.

- *Ensuring children know how the guardian will inform the court about their wishes and feelings.* If children are not able or willing to make their own contribution to the guardian's report (through writing or pictures), they need to be confident about what the guardian will write or say. Wherever possible they should be shown the relevant parts of the guardian's report.

- *Seeing children alone.* Most guardians always see children on their own at least once if not more often during the course of proceedings, but this research illustrates that this good practice needs emphasising. The one case where a contact order was recommended by a guardian without seeing the child is hard to understand, and links with comments about complaints and grievance, below. There are also links with how the children are prepared for sessions with their guardians and how they can contribute to the guardian's report.

- *Ensuring the children know the guardian's views.* Most children believed their guardian knew their wishes and feelings and where these differed from the guardian's recommendations about their best interest they understood the reasoning. However, some were uncertain and were troubled by this. Given the guardian's unique position and specific duties to safeguard welfare, it seems reasonable to suggest that the guardian should check that the child understands.

- *Ensuring discussion and planning about seeing the court or attending the hearing.* Not all the children wished to see or attend the court, but the children who felt excluded from the court process had strong feelings about this and illustrated graphically their need to have more involvement in the process. There is also a link to the point made about being satisfied that the court really knows their wishes and feelings. One could hypothesise that the guardians who take the time to take children to see the court are also the ones in whom the children have confidence about representing their views.

- *Ensuring the children learn of the decisions made at court/good-bye visit.* The research has illustrated the children's good ability to understand the significance of court orders for them. They need to know when final orders are made and understand that the guardian will no longer be coming to see them. It may not be possible for a good-bye visit to occur immediately, but the children in this sample describe how important such a visit is, a point which was reinforced by visits which failed to occur.

- *Ensuring children know about complaints and grievance procedures.* This is about empowering children and ensuring good practice. Adults involved in the proceedings should also know of these – details are in the explanatory leaflets. This applies to the process of the work, not to the recommendation itself, which should be challenged if necessary in court, i.e. it is about the way the work is done, or not done.

## OPPORTUNITIES FOR CHILDREN

- *Having the opportunity to contribute to the guardian's report.* This links with the guardian ensuring the child knows that wishes and feelings must be considered as part of the decision-making. One suggestion is that older children seen in secure accommodation proceedings, where time is short, could contribute to a draft of relevant sections.

- *Having the opportunity to see parts of the guardian's report.* This would ensure that children knew exactly what the guardian was writing down on their behalf, and where wishes and feelings differ from an assessment of best interests (safeguarding welfare) at least some of the reasons for this.

- *Having the opportunity to see the court or attend hearings.* This is about involving children in the process and allaying some of their concerns or fantasies.

- *Developing a system for feedback from children.* The views of children provided this research project with a wealth of information, from which we hope guardians and others will learn. As a further means of empowering children and maintaining good practice, a simple feedback system would contribute to the monitoring of practice. It could be incorporated into the existing system of appraisal for guardians, which is likely to be incorporated into the new service.

## IMPLICATIONS FOR POLICY

The maintenance and development of good practice is linked with quality assurance. Reference has been made to the continuation of guardians *ad litem* within the new Children and Family Court Advisory Service, and to the discussion about whether party status for children will continue to be automatic with the right to be represented by a Children Panel solicitor. If the unique partnership of guardians and solicitors is to continue in public law proceedings, it is also necessary to ensure that high standards of practice are maintained. Simply having the structure is not enough and safeguards are also needed so that as far as possible the best recommendations are made in what are often very complex circumstances.

In amalgamating the guardian service with the court welfare service (and official solicitor service) it is hoped that in due course skills will merge. There are arguments about whether some children in private law proceedings should be more carefully assessed and also have party status (something which can occur at present, but rarely). This implies a levelling up rather than a levelling down. Currently the court welfare service carries a heavy workload and emphasis is given to meditation where possible. There has been an assumption in private law that contact with both parents should be pursued wherever possible and that this best promotes welfare. This potentially carries great risks for children where family violence is an issue. The assumption is questioned by many guardians and others working with or researching family violence, who would alternatively propose that safety comes first. For some within the new service this may imply a move away from an agreement-focused approach towards a safety-orientated approach with domestic violence being seen as a child protection issue. We would note that the latter is likely to involve a lengthier assessment and the development of high levels of communication skills for working with children. However, this would be a fairer system. The skills developed by guardians for negotiating and mediating between professionals, and between professionals and parents during the course of proceedings need to be acknowledged, as this less tangible contribution, demonstrated in the research of professionals' views, will be of value in the new service. The new service offers many opportunities to children as long as these issues are addressed.

## CONCLUSION

These two research studies emphasise the need to maintain an independent, informed, child-focused service. The research on children's views illustrated how children can understand quite complex systems and processes relevant to them; can be given the opportunity to become involved according to their own needs and wishes; and make informed choices. They valued their guardians for listening to them, explaining decision-making, and placing responsibility for decision-making with the adults, and particularly the courts. Being enabled to express their wishes and feelings and so contribute to the process effectively helped them to feel empowered.

These important decisions are about the children and their futures. It is vital that children are given information so they can make an informed decision about the level of their own involvement and the alternatives available to them, not only in the process but also in the final decisions and their implications. This links with the principles of the European Convention and the United Nations Convention on the Rights of the Child (1989).

Both studies emphasise the valued part of the guardian's role in representing children's views which is such a crucial part of the decision-making. This kept the focus on the child, enabling a service to the courts also to be a service for children.

# *Appendix 1*

LOCAL AUTHORITY PROFILE OF TWO RESEARCH SAMPLES

*RESEARCH ON CHILDREN'S VIEWS*

**Table 7** *Proportion of cases completed by local authority for children's research sample and Humberside Panel over same period*

| Local authority | Sample of children interviewed (*N* = 19 cases) (%) | Humberside GALRO Panel Jun 1998–Dec 1998* (*N* = 210 cases) (%) |
|---|---|---|
| Kingston upon Hull | 10 (53%) | 108 (51%) |
| East Riding of Yorkshire | 4 (21%) | 39 (19%) |
| North Lincolnshire | 4 (21%) | 32 (15%) |
| North East Lincolnshire | 1 (5%) | 31 (15%) |

*Period of data collection for children's research.

*RESEARCH ON PROFESSIONALS' VIEWS*

**Table 8** *Proportion of cases completed by local authority for professionals' research sample and Humberside Panel over same period*

| Local authority | Sample of cases (*N* = 21 cases) (%) | Humberside GALRO Panel Sept 1997–Feb 1998** (*N* = 150 cases) (%) |
|---|---|---|
| Kingston upon Hull | 13 (62%) | 73 (49%) |
| East Riding of Yorkshire | 3 (14%) | 28 (18.5%) |
| North Lincolnshire | 2 (10%) | 21 (14%) |
| North East Lincolnshire | 3 (14%) | 28 (18.5%) |

**Period of data collection for professionals' research.

# *Appendix 2*

PARTICIPATION RATES FOR CHILDREN'S RESEARCH

**Table 9** *Participation rates by gender, local authority, type of proceeding, and person living with child*

| | Children Interviewed | Children not interviewed | | | Total |
| --- | --- | --- | --- | --- | --- |
| | | Do not approach children on recommendation of GAL and SW | Unresponsive | Actively refused to participate | |
| | (%) | (%) | (%) | (%) | |
| **Gender:** | | | | | |
| Male | 12 (42.8) | 5 (29.4) | 9 (50) | 13 (65) | 39 |
| Female | 16 (57.2) | 12 (70.6) | 9 (50) | 7 (35) | 44 |
| **Living with:** | | | | | |
| Parent/s | 9 (32.1) | 11 (64.7) | 12 (66.7) | 10 (50) | 42 |
| Other relative | 4 (14.3) | 1 (5.9) | 0 | 3 (15) | 8 |
| Fostercare | 11 (39.3) | 1 (5.9) | 2 (11.1) | 6 (30) | 20 |
| Residential/ secure accom. | 4 (14.3) | 4 (23.5) | 4 (22.2) | 1 (5) | 13 |
| **LA:** | | | | | |
| Kingston upon Hull | 16 (57.1) | 10 (58.8) | 10 (55.5) | 13 (65) | 49 |
| East Riding | 5 (17.9) | 0 | 5 (27.8) | 2 (10) | 12 |
| North Lincolnshire | 5 (17.9) | 1 (5.9) | 0 | 3 (15) | 9 |
| North East Lincolnshire | 2 (7.1) | 4 (23.5) | 3 (16.7) | 2 (10) | 11 |
| Other | 0 | 2 (11.8) | 0 | 0 | 2 |
| **Type of proceeding at application:** | | | | | |
| Section 31 orders | 22 | 13 | 13 | 16 | 64 |
| Other orders | 4 | 3 | 3 | 4 | 14 |
| Secure order | 2 | 1 | 2 | 0 | 5 |
| **Total number of children in each group** | | | | | |
| | 28 | 17 | 18 | 20 | 83 |

# *Appendix 3*

CHILDREN'S RESEARCH 'IDEAL' CARD GAME FIGURES BY AGE AND GENDER

**Table 10** *Top two characteristics of an ideal guardian chosen by age*

| An 'ideal' guardian most importantly should (be) ... | 8- to 11-year-olds N=17 children* (%) | 12- to 17-year-olds N=10 children (%) | Combined age groups N=27 children* (%) |
|---|---|---|---|
| Listen | 13 (38%) | 7 (35%) | 20 (37%) |
| Explain things to you | 7 (21%) | 5 (25%) | 12 (22%) |
| Helpful | 3 (9%) | 2 (10%) | 5 (9%) |
| Give you time when you want it | 3 (9%) | 1 (5%) | 4 (7%) |
| Kind | 3 (9%) | 1 (5%) | 4 (7%) |
| Easy to talk to | 2 (5.5%) | 1 (5%) | 3 (6%) |
| Get things done | 2 (5.5%) | 1 (5%) | 3 (6%) |
| Is interested in you | 1 (3%) | 2 (10%) | 3 (6%) |
| **Total**** | **34** | **20** | **54** |

*One child did not complete this task.
**Two cards were chosen by each child or young person.

**Table 11** *Top two characteristics of an ideal guardian for boys and girls*

| An 'ideal' guardian most importantly should (be)... | Boys N=11 children (%) | Girls N=16 children (%) |
|---|---|---|
| Listen | 7 (32%) | 13 (41%) |
| Explain things to you | 4 (18%) | 8 (25%) |
| Helpful | 3 (14%) | 2 (6.25%) |
| Give you time when you want it | 0 | 4 (12.5%) |
| Kind | 3 (14%) | 1 (3%) |
| Easy to talk to | 1 (4.5%) | 2 (6.25%) |
| Get things done | 2 (9%) | 1 (3%) |
| Is interested in you | 2 (9%) | 1 (3%) |
| **Total** | **22** | **32** |

# References

Alderson, P. (1995) *Listening to Children: Children, Ethics and Social Research*. London: Barnardo's.

Backett, K. and Alexander, H. (1991) 'Talking to young children about health: methods and findings.' *Health Education Journal*, **50**(1), pp. 34–38.

Beresford, B. (1997) *Personal Accounts: Involving Disabled Children in Research*. Norwich: Social Policy Research Unit.

Children Act Advisory Committee (1997) *Handbook of Best Practice in Children Act Cases*. London: Children Act Advisory Committee.

Clark, D. J. (1995) *Whose Case is it Anyway?* Master of Philosophy Thesis, University of Sussex.

Clark, A. and Sinclair, R. (1999) *The Child in Focus: The Evolving Role of the Guardian* ad Litem. London: NCB.

Department of Health and Social Security (1974) *Report of the Committee of Inquiry into the Care and Supervision Provided in Relation to Maria Colwell*. London: HMSO.

Department of Health (1992) *Manual of Practice Guidance for Guardians* ad Litem *and Reporting Officers*. London: HMSO.

Department of Health/Welsh Office (1995) *National Standards for the Guardian* ad Litem *and Reporting Officer Service*. London: HMSO.

Department of Health (1996) *Implementing National Standards: A Guide Through Quality Assurance for the Guardian Service*. London: HMSO.

The Family Proceedings Rules (1991) London: HMSO.

Garbarino, J., Scott, F. M. and Erikson Institute (1992) *What Children Can Tell Us*. Jossey-Bass: San Francisco.

Hansard (1996) Lord Irvine of Lairg in the House of Lords, Debate on the Family, 11 December 1996, at pp. 1093–1095.

Hill, M., Laybourn, A. and Borland, M. (1996) 'Engaging with primary-aged children about their emotions and well-being: methodological considerations.' *Children and Society*, **10**, pp. 129–144.

Home Office (1994) *National Standards for Probation Service Family Court Welfare Work*. London: HMSO.

Hood, S., Kelley, P. and Mayall, B. (1996) Children as research subjects: a risky enterprise. *Children and Society*, **10**, pp. 117–128.

Hunt, J. and Murch, M. (1990) *Speaking Out for Children*. London: The Children's Society.

Kerr, A. and Gregory, E. (1998) *The Work of the Guardian* ad Litem*: Practitioner's Guide*. Birmingham: Venture Press.

Koocher, G. and Keith-Spiegel, P. (1994) 'Scientific issues on psychosocial and educational research with children.' In M.A. Grodin and L.H. Glantz (eds) *Children as Research Subjects: Science, Ethics and Law*. New York: Oxford University Press.

Levin, I. (1994) 'Children's perceptions of their family.' In J. Brannen and M. O'Brien (eds) *Childhood and Parenthood: Proceedings of the International Sociological Association Committee for Family Research Conference*. Institute of Education, London: University of London.

Mahon, A., Glendinning, C., Clarke, K. and Craig, G. (1996) 'Researching children: Methods and ethics.' *Children and Society*, **10**, pp. 145–154.

Masson, J. and Winn Oakley, M. (1999) *Out of Hearing: Representing Children in Care Proceedings*. NSPCC: Wiley.

Mauthner, M. (1997) 'Methodological aspects of collecting data from children: Lessons from three research projects.' *Children and Society*, **11**, pp. 16–28.

Murch, M., Hunt, J. and MacLeod, A. (1990) *The Representation of the Child in Civil Proceedings Research Project 1985–89: Summary of Conclusions and Recommendations for the Department of Health*. Socio-Legal Centre for Family Studies: University of Bristol.

Oakley, A., Bendelow, G., Barnes, J., Buchanan, M. and Hussain, O. A. N. (1995) 'Health and cancer prevention: knowledge and beliefs of children and young people.' *British Medical Journal*, **310**, pp. 1029–1033.

Social Services Inspectorate (1990) *In the Interests of Children: An Inspection of the Guardian* ad Litem *and Reporting Officer Service*. London: HMSO.

Tammivaara, J. and Enright, S. (1986) 'On eliciting information: dialogues with child informants.' *Anthropology and Education Quarterly*, **17**, pp. 218–238.

Timmis, G. (1996) What's the good of a Guardian? *Representing Children*, **9**, pp. 226–243.

Timms, J. E. (1995) *Children's Representation: A Practitioner's Guide*. London: Sweet and Maxwell.

Weber, L.R., Miracle, A. and Skehan, T. (1994) 'Interviewing early adolescents: some methodological considerations.' *Human Organization*, **53**(1), pp. 42–47.

# THE CHILDREN'S SOCIETY
*A POSITIVE FORCE FOR CHANGE*

The Children's Society is one of Britain's leading charities for children and young people. Founded in 1881 as a Christian organisation, The Children's Society reaches out unconditionally to children and young people regardless of race, culture or creed.

### Over 90 projects throughout England and Wales
We work with over 30,000 children of all ages, focusing on those whose circumstances have made them particularly vulnerable. We aim to help stop the spiral into isolation, anger and lost hope faced by so many young people.

### We constantly look for effective, new ways of making a real difference
We measure local impact and demonstrate through successful practice that major issues can be tackled and better resolved. The Children's Society has an established track record of taking effective action: both in changing public perceptions about difficult issues such as child prostitution, and in influencing national policy and practice to give young people a better chance at life.

### The Children's Society is committed to overcoming injustice wherever we find it
We are currently working towards national solutions to social isolation, lack of education and the long-term problems they cause, through focused work in several areas:

- helping parents whose babies and toddlers have inexplicably stopped eating, endangering their development;
- involving children in the regeneration of poorer communities;
- preventing exclusions from primary and secondary schools;
- providing a safety net for young people who run away from home and care;
- seeking viable alternatives to the damaging effects of prison for young offenders.

The Children's Society will continue to raise public awareness of difficult issues to promote a fairer society for the most vulnerable children in England and Wales. For further information about the work of The Children's Society or to obtain a publications catalogue, please contact:

The Children's Society, Publishing Department, Edward Rudolf House, Margery Street, London WC1X 0JL. Tel. 020 7841 4400. Fax 020 7841 4500. Website: www.the-childrens-society.org.uk

The Children's Society is a registered charity: Charity Registration No. 221124.